Making Places for F

M000204477

Making Places for People explores twelve social questions
environmental design. Authors Christie Johnson Coffin and Jenny
Young bring perspectives from practice and teaching to challenge
assumptions about how places meet human needs. The book
reveals deeper complexities in addressing basic questions, such as:
What is the story of this place? What logic orders it? How big is it?
How sustainable is it? Providing an overview of a growing body of
knowledge about people and places, *Making Places for People*
stimulates curiosity and further discussion. The authors argue that
critical understanding of the relationships between people and their
built environments can inspire designs that better contribute to
health, human performance, and social equity—bringing meaning
and delight to people's lives.

Christie Johnson Coffin practices architecture in the Western United
States and internationally in Taiwan, India, and Nicaragua, with a
focus on social design for health-care and research laboratory
buildings. Her university teaching includes the University of
California, Berkeley, the Massachusetts Institute of Technology,
California Polytechnic University, and the University of Oregon. She
is the co-author of *Changing Hospital Environments for Children.*

Jenny Young teaches design and human factors in design. Her
research on small town development focuses on the roles public
buildings play in town stability and vitality. Her architectural
practice includes consulting on schools, libraries, clinics, and
designing residential projects. She is Professor of Architecture at
the University of Oregon.

"Creating environments that enable a diverse cross-section of people to thrive requires attention to human psychological and behavioral processes and physical needs. By expounding on twelve key design-focused questions, *Making Places for People* weaves a narrative of environmental design theory and techniques to enrich human experience, while referencing important works of architecture and planning from around the world. The book provides a framework for understanding how well designed built form can support healthy communities and foster human well-being."

Dr. Lynne M. Dearborn, AIA, Associate Professor of Architecture, University of Illinois at Urbana-Champaign, USA

Making Places for People

12 Questions Every Designer Should Ask

Christie Johnson Coffin
and
Jenny Young

Routledge
Taylor & Francis Group

NEW YORK AND LONDON

First published 2017
by Routledge
711 Third Avenue, New York, NY 10017

and by Routledge
2 Park Square, Milton Park, Abingdon, Oxon OX14 4RN

Routledge is an imprint of the Taylor & Francis Group, an informa business

Library of Congress Cataloguing in Publication Data
Names: Coffin, Christie, author. I Young, Jenny (Jenny E.), author.
Title: Making places for people : 12 questions every designer should ask /
Christie Johnson Coffin and Jenny Young.
Description: New York : Routledge, 2017. I
Includes bibliographical references and index.
Identifiers: LCCN 2016022823I ISBN 9781138860636 (hb : alk. paper) I
ISBN 9781138860643 (pb : alk. paper) I ISBN 9781315716374 (ebook)
Subjects: LCSH: Architecture—Human factors. I Architecture and society. I
Architectural design.
Classification: LCC NA2542.4 .C64 2016 I DDC 720.1/03—dc23
LC record available at https://lccn.loc.gov/2016022823

ISBN: 978-1-138-86063-6 (hbk)
ISBN: 978-1-138-86064-3 (pbk)
ISBN: 978-1-315-71637-4 (ebk)

Acquisition Editor: Wendy Fuller
Editorial Assistant: Trudy Varcianna
Production Editor: Alanna Donaldson

Typeset in New Century Schoolbook and Trade Gothic
by Florence Production Ltd, Stoodleigh, Devon, UK

Contents

Acknowledgments

We cannot hope to mention personally the many architects, planners, designers, landscape architects, scientists, physicians, teachers, professors, students, friends, and family members who have worked with us and challenged us with their questions. We would especially like to thank the Tom and Carol Williams Fund for Undergraduate Education at the University of Oregon whose grant to develop and enrich the required lecture course "Human Context of Design" started us on the road to this book.

Teachers and colleagues to whom we are particularly indebted include Jeh Johnson at Vassar College, Dorothy Lee at Radcliffe/Harvard College, Christopher Alexander, Roslyn Lindheim, and Ray Lifchez at Berkeley, and at the University of Oregon, Howard Davis, Gunilla Finrow, Jerry Finrow, Bill Gilland, Joanne Hogarth, Peter Keyes, Michael Pease, David Rowe, John Rowell, and Fred Tepfer. We offer special thanks to Mark Gillem, Linda Zimmer, and Christina Bollo, who co-taught Human Context with us, and to the many students who engaged with these questions and contributed to the joy of teaching.

We became architects because of a love of the tangible, of making real places for people. It has been a privilege to work with practices that have a commitment to social projects, even on limited budgets: in the San Francisco Bay area, the Center for Environmental Structure, the Design Partnership, KMD, Ratcliff Architects, and SMP; in Eugene, Oregon, Rowell Brokaw Architects; in Taipei, Taiwan, EDS

International and National Taiwan University Building and Planning Foundation.

Thanks to the many people who have helped us put this book together. We are grateful to Professor Alison Kwok who connected us to our editors, and to Wendy Fuller, Alanna Donaldson, Graham Frankland, Grace Harrison, Naomi Hill, and Trudy Varcianna, who have guided us through the process at Routledge. Special thanks to Julie West Johnson for her fine early edit and encouragement, and to Michael Caleb Lester for expert copyediting.

Many friends and colleagues provided beautiful photographs and illustrations: John Boerger, Christina Bollo, Mike Burns, Peter Clegg, Stephen Coffin, Donald Corner, Howard Davis, Jerry Finrow, Christopher Grubbs, Megan Haight, Amanda Hansen, Bill Hocker, Noelle E. Jones, Kaarin Knudson, Alison Kwok, Kit Larsen, Lisa McClellan, John Rowell, Studio Gang, MeiLi Xiao. We only wish we could use them all.

We are grateful to many who have shared ideas and articles: Katherine Anderson, Laura de la Torre Bueno, Yung Ling Chen, Nga Dao, David Davies, Howard Davis, Chang Lin Dillingham, Nancy Florence, Mark and Megan Haight, John K. C. Liu, Carol Mancke, Patti Quinn, Jerry Reynolds, Henry Sanoff, Yuan-Liang Tsai, Jun-Li Wang, and Judith Wasserman.

We are indebted to our families for their love and support, our parents Edmund and Lillian Christie Johnson and Irwin and Edith Proctor Young, Margia, James and Elizabeth, Jesse and Joan, Walker, William, Carol and Ken, Julie and Lance, Leslie and Jerry, and, of course, our husbands Stephen Coffin and Donald Corner.

All ideas and assertions that readers may question, we alone own. If people are motivated to react, correct and improve and build on what we have laid out in these explorations, we will feel we have in some way fulfilled our intentions.

Berkeley Art Museum and Pacific Film Archive, Diller, Scofidio + Renfro Architects,
Stephen Coffin, photographer

Introduction

It's hard to design a space that will not attract people.
What is remarkable is how often this has been
accomplished.[1]

William H. Whyte

Architecture is fundamentally about people. Questions about
the role of place in human life are central to our work as
architects, university teachers, and researchers. We try to
awaken in our students, clients, and colleagues the ability to
question and seek understanding of how built form can
support individuals, foster communities, and enrich human
lives.

We bring different perspectives. Christie is a practicing
architect, who has done research and teaching, and Jenny is
a professor of architecture, who has done research and
practice. The process of working together on this book started
with co-teaching a required lecture class called "The Human
Context of Design" in the School of Architecture and Allied
Arts at the University of Oregon. We were joined each year
by graduate teaching fellows, who assisted us in teaching,
and hundreds of design students early in their education,
who were full of questions. They too brought different
perspectives.

Environmental behavior studies became prominent in
architectural discourse in the 1960s. We took our professional
degrees at the University of California, Berkeley, one center
of this thinking. The civil rights movement, the women's
movement, and the anti-war movement were subtexts to

educational activity in Berkeley at the time. As young professionals, we sought improvements in social institutions, using architecture as a tool. Designing housing in Peru and Mexico, working on hospital, clinic, and school projects—we questioned everything.

At that time of social unrest, people reassessed whether institutions were, in fact, working towards the humane and democratic goals they professed. Fashionable buildings of the era were criticized as "hard" buildings, more about power and control than about people. Environments built for cars and suburban development were seen as undermining traditional urban centers and draining them of vitality. Reaction to these trends led to an outpouring of research about the relationships between environments and human behavior.

The classics of environment-behavior literature emerged in the 1960s and 1970s and included work by Jane Jacobs, Edward Hall, Roger Barker, Kevin Lynch, Christopher Alexander, Robert Sommer, Erving Goffman, Oscar Newman, Jon Lang, Roslyn Lindheim, Clare Cooper Marcus, and many others. Ways to use what was being learned emerged in design patterns, guidelines, and checklists. Models developed at that time are still in use today.

Knowledge in the field has continued to grow, but it has faded from the forefront. Few architecture books today focus on people and communities, although the Environmental Design Research Association continues to encourage and publish this work. In many design schools, social design is a distant third after sculptural expression and green technologies. Social and psychological issues are not thought of as fertile form generators.

There are signs of renewed interest in the potential of design where concerns about the human condition are primary. Public health, planning, and geography have taken up research that adds to our understanding of the built environment. Young professionals are anxious to use their capabilities for the 99 percent of the world's population not served by traditional design professions. Designers have renewed commitment to learning from past experience to make places that are better for people. Building renovation and reuse is becoming a larger component of practice, offering clear evidence of ways that places do or do not solve human needs over time. Evidence-based design initiatives are emerging.

This book gives an overview of a growing body of knowledge and provides a resource to inform conversation among designers, owners, building committee members, and students of design about interactions among places and people.

We continue to question. We present here twelve questions; it could be twenty. These twelve questions are widely varied and include questions every designer and client should ask. These questions are what Horst Rittel called "wicked questions,"[2] questions with no easy and no single answers. Tame questions have correct answers, although not everyone will get the right answer every time. When we ask "How big is this place?" we find that a simple answer like 100 square meters is not enough. Size and scale affect people in a wide variety of ways. We offer a window into some of the available thinking and research, but we want readers to think about these questions and add their own.

We address these questions to activate curiosity and to provoke thought about the relationships among people in all their diversity and the places they inhabit. We address these questions not so much to provide final answers, but to bring to the table evidence that can be employed in seeking answers. In some cases the evidence is very slim. We know a little about a lot of things.

Untangling the links between place and social life is complex. At the same time, it brings with it the reward of generating places that contribute more fully to human performance, health, and social equity—bringing meaning and delight to people's lives. We dedicate this book to building understanding of how to make better places for people.

Notes

1   William H. Whyte, "Quotable," Project for Public Spaces. Retrieved August 23, 2016 at: www.pps.org/reference/wwhyte.

2   Horst Rittel as discussed in Jon Kolko, *Wicked Problems: Problems Worth Solving* (Austin, TX: Austin Center for Design, 2012). Excerpt online in *Stanford Social Innovation Review*, March 6, 2012. Retrieved August 23, 2016 at: http://ssir.org/articles/entry/wicked_problems_problems_worth_solving.

Figure 1.1
Taj Mahal, Agra, India, Howard Davis, photographer

Chapter 1
What is the Story
of this Place?

What distinguishes the worst architect from the best of
bees is this, that the architect raises ... structure in
imagination before ... erect[ing] it in reality.[1]

Karl Marx

Narrative has always been a common thread for
understanding human experience, a thread that connects
events in words. Narratives, or stories, can coalesce setting,
personalities, and action, as well as add meaning and even a
symbolic or poetic layer to design thought. Stories are told in
prose and poetry, song, theater, and dance, in still and
moving images. Built places tell stories in various forms and
can emphasize different elements: place, concept, people, or
action. Narratives of built places can be practical or
metaphorical, non-fiction or fiction.

The last chapter in a love story, the Taj Mahal is a tomb
built by Mughal Emperor Shah Jahan in memory of his third
wife, the Persian princess Mumtaz Mahal, who died at the
birth of their fourteenth child.[2] Exquisite in form and detail,
the white marble tomb, with its iconic onion dome, its corners
framed by four minarets, stands inside a walled garden
complex. Following the Islamic prohibition of using
anthropometric forms, its fine decorations derive from
calligraphy and vegetative motifs. Ironically, it stands no
longer in a Mughal empire but in a mainly Hindu country.

Two recent claims that the Taj Mahal was built by a Hindu king were both dismissed by the Indian Supreme Court.[3]

Brasilia is the story of a new town built to recognize a new republic and bring a less known and less urbanized part of the country into prominence. Proposed in 1827 by Emperor Pedro I's advisor José Bonifácio, the new capital was not put into practice until the mid-twentieth century by President Juscelino Kubitschek, who promised it in his campaign as part of a story about creating fifty years of prosperity in five years. Modernist architect Oscar Niemeyer and landscape architect Roberto Burle Marx organized elements of the new city in the shape of an airplane, a key symbol of contemporary life and one of many stories behind this new town.

Architects Polly Cooper and Ken Haggard's Trout Farm outside Santa Margarita, California, tells a story of rebuilding resourcefully after a major forest fire. On the edge of a national forest, the original house and a broad mix of deciduous trees burned. The trees were in essence kiln-dried by the fire. A portable mill was brought on-site, and the trees became lumber for the structure and millwork for a new off-the-grid straw bale house, the San Luis Obispo Solar Group's office, and a workshop dubbed "the tool temple." The resulting complex, which includes several ponds from an ancient failed trout farm, is a wonderful place for large or small groups of people, making music, eating, working, or just watching the wildlife and seasons pass.

The Vietnam Veterans Memorial tells the story of a war that scarred two nations. It was not designed by a professional group but by young architecture student Maya Lin who won a national competition. From the first, visitors have used it to tell their own stories of a loved one lost, a generation damaged, a sacrifice made.

Many have seen pictures of the Vietnam Veterans Memorial and read about it, but experiencing a place is always something different. The Memorial is a wound, like

Figure 1.2
Vietnam Veterans Memorial, Washington, D.C., Maya Lin, architect, Mike Burns, photographer

war, a cut in the green lawn of the Washington Mall. One descends into the earth, as the dead must, along a reflective black marble wall flush with the lawn. The wall grows as you go down. Names of the dead are inscribed, organized by date of death, so there are few at the beginning, but as you go deeper and the wall grows higher, there are more and more names. The names are embedded in black marble slabs that reflect the living, the sky, and the trees of the world with an otherworldly eeriness.

Then there is a turning point, as all wars have turning points. In the Memorial it is an obtuse angle, where there are the most names, and there you turn and begin to ascend. As the wall grows shorter and the number of names decreases, you rise until there is no more wall and you are on the surface of the Mall, facing the Washington Monument, again part of the living, but remembering all the sacrifices made.[4]

From the first, the Vietnam Veterans Memorial has drawn people to it. Some come to look, some to pay homage to the loss of so many, and many to leave flowers or notes or remembrances. Every design decision made, from the shape made by the wall dug into the earth to the materials and their detailing, intensifies those human experiences. When she lectures, Maya Lin describes how she designs to tell the story and give the facts—not tell people what to feel—so people can react personally.[5]

Place

In all of these stories, place, concept, people, and action play a part. A story that focuses on place attends to the context and fabric of the environment. In the simplest sense, this can be the story of travels, like a picaresque novel. Designers often envision moving around a new environment, telling stories of a spatial unfolding, as a person walks through space from place to place. Curiously, these stories typically focus on entering a place and seldom include the experience of leaving the place. They focus inwards. Many tell the story of entering the Taj Mahal, but who remembers the story of leaving and reentering the fascinating and chaotic city. Active moving through space may add coherence, taking precedence over humdrum day-after-day use or less cinematic lingering.

In this type of narrative, a place is the star of a story featuring encountering, entering, and exploring a landscape, urban fabric, or building. When Paul Ma designed destination resorts, he learned from the film industry. With illustrator Christopher Grubbs, he developed actual storyboards that detailed events in a resort visit, starting with the glass of juice offered by the innkeeper in the entry garden and including the (optional) swim with dolphins. The storyboard, illustrated by small but detailed sketches of

What is the Story of this Place?

Figure 1.3
Storyboard Sketches for a Resort, Christopher Grubbs, illustrator

each event, became the program for building the resort. The episodic experience of the environment formed a key thread.[6]

Concept

The concept story is more abstract and focuses on problem solving or new thinking. The story is a quest. It asks a question, seeks an answer, and then solves the problem. The narrative may be driven by a concrete concept, such as meeting net zero energy guidelines; a social goal, such as supporting healthy adolescent behavior; or even a metaphor, such as "This place is a harbor for people in crisis." The question can be a negative one, such as "How can this place be less institutional?" or a positive one, such as "How can this place be friendlier?" It may be poetic: "Can this place be like inhabiting a cloud?" It can be very practical: "Can this place be so easy to clean it can just be hosed down?" Seeking an elegant solution is the essential narrative.

Taiwanese community planner and architect John K. C. Liu talks about aboriginal Taiwanese, who were forced to relocate to escape landslides that inundated their town. Residents sought to replicate part of the old place by recreating a significant and very large rock in plastic. They made an exact mold from the original rock and cast a hollow plastic rock in the new town. Liu questioned whether the hollow replica could carry the history and idea of the original, but the villagers repeated many stories that the rock brought with it and attested to its effective place in the narrative of their town. The replica carried the story of the rock, adding meaning and substance to their resettled town.

The place itself may not be the focus. The emphasis may be on ideas the project can represent. The design of the place may concentrate on advancing knowledge in a more general sense or on supporting cultural practices or values. Student assignments in architecture school often focus on theoretical quests. Indeed, some built forms embody abstract concept stories, such as Diller, Scofidio + Renfro's Blur Building for the Swiss National Expo.[7]

People

In people stories, people come first and are clothed in appropriate places. Stories infuse places with the characters that commission and inhabit landscapes and buildings. The narrative can be a type of coming-of-age story or *Bildungsroman*. People may be at a crossroads, where something new and interesting can happen. Designers often tell stories about how the building will adapt, enrich, or change lives. Adding daylight will lift morale and increase productivity. A more compact hospital plan will eliminate many steps each day and provide more time for caregiving. An improved factory layout will improve productivity and reduce errors. Parks will bring people into the public realm and improve health. A new home will mend a failing marriage. Some of these narratives are fiction and some non-fiction. Stories can provide a clear narrative structure with plots and subplots for a place.

Embellishments to the narrative frequently include eccentricities of the characters, such as the need for a large safe in the manager's office to keep clients' valuables in a Mayo Clinic program used by foreign billionaires. In an early childhood education center in eastern Oregon, the architects named the interior paint "Donna's blue" for the director who selected it to provide a unifying and calming environment. Hooks for hanging bicycles from the ceiling are showing up in workplaces of young athletic professionals. The practice of *taiji* can inspire the development of a level spot surrounded by significant trees. The life of individual people defines the fabric of these stories and may be used creatively.

Sociologist Russ Ellis and architecture theorist Dana Cuff have written about "architects' people," the characters that designers imagine, as they form the narrative for a building.[8] These people are often compelling and interesting, but sometimes say more about the designer than the future building users. Architect Le Corbusier invented a person to inhabit his buildings, the modulor, and later developed an improved, taller modulor.[9] The system of measurements was based on the golden ratio (1:1.62), long thought a graceful proportion by Western architects. It has been noted: no modulor woman. American airplane seats designed to meet the dimensions of 95 percent of American men do not meet the needs of 95 percent of American women. Men as a proxy for women in size and shape is a flawed narrative.

Action

The action story focuses on the fabric of the world in need of mending or improvement. For this narrative model, people may see built form as a part of a stream of history, and as having an influence on that history. A historic building may be challenged, or alternately, a historic pattern may be failing and in need of change to achieve relevance for contemporary life. Le Corbusier created a classic story that has become a part of the rationalism of the modern movement: "Une maison est une machine-à-habiter," or, "A house is a machine for living in."[10] For his Unité d'habitation he worked with designer Charlotte Perriand to make kitchens that are a testament to this rationalism. Each part of the kitchen was designed in detail to meet the needs of a French cook.[11]

These aspirational stories are often part of new urban design, where growth and change in the city has left the old culture scattered and a new culture is emerging. Utopian and practical planners have long sought to reimagine the city to better support humanity. Ebenezer Howard's Garden City, Frederick Law Olmsted's urban parks, and Pierre Charles L'Enfant's Washington, DC plan are among these plans that can still be seen today. Frank Lloyd Wright's Broadacre City was an important model for American suburbs.

The Value of Narrative

These narratives weave together elements of the built environment to make the larger universe of places whole, safe, and attractive. These stories inevitably involve places, people, actions, and concepts in differing degrees. The value of narrative in design is often at the heart of designing itself. Are these stories factual or merely a useful tool for organizing collective thought about place and ordering creative thinking? Stories certainly can bring into focus what has come to be called "the vision" for the enterprise of changing the built environment. Nigel Coates discusses how architects as diverse as William Kent, who designed Chiswick House, Antoni Gaudí, who dreamed the Sagrada Família Cathedral that is still under construction, and Rem Koolhaas, who switched from scriptwriting to architecture, have effectively used narrative to create coherent understandings in a complex multifaceted world.[12] On the other hand, different people in the same place at the same time may tell various stories, not unlike the differences in story revealed by different observers in the movie *Rashomon*.[13] The nature of the narrative, brief, or program that orders a new place affects the conversation during design and the direction the built form takes.

What is the story that you tell yourself about a place you are designing? Do you imagine the building or open space filled with people, or do you imagine a setting by itself before the people arrive? How do you connect your ideas for a place with all the people who will ultimately inhabit it? Do you imagine what it will be like in twenty years? Do you imagine the place improving over time?

Community members involved in planning new places can often tell stories about what is will be like when the place is complete. These stories can offer very human inspiration for design. Some stories can be extremely short. In one discussion, a building committee was asked to imagine that everything was built and the place was just wonderful. What would it be like? A key member of the community said very simply, "peaceful." The conversation stopped abruptly and everyone thought for a minute. Other committee members said "yes." But what did "peaceful" mean to each person? Part of the conversation of design is listening to others' stories, then blending and integrating these stories to make a layered and more interesting whole.

Sometimes the best intentions do not work out, and places go on to have different stories. The Museum of the Struggle at Red Location was built in Port Elizabeth, South Africa, at the oldest surviving site where thousands of native Africans were forced to settle by the colonial government in the early 1900s.[14] Red Location became a center of resistance during apartheid. After apartheid ended in 1994, Noero Wolff Architects were hired to develop a cultural precinct in the center of the township. The project set out to make a place telling the story of apartheid by building a museum and at the same time a center for the community. The plan was that the museum would attract visitors, provide jobs, and build the economy. In front of the museum and around it, Noero Wolff designed a plaza as the hub of a new zone with housing, an arts center, and a library. In consultation with the local population, the Phase I museum and its plaza were designed and built. The small memory boxes, in which families kept their most precious things as they moved from place to place, inspired the designers to organize the building around a set of twelve large-scale memory boxes, vertical, top-lit rooms in which to tell different stories of the

Figure 1.4
Museum at Red Location, Naero Wolff Architects, Iwan Baan, photographer

resistance. The building stands out in scale from the one-story ramshackle houses, but in character it reflects the industrial heritage of the area with repeating roof forms and straightforward materials of concrete block and metal siding.

Unexpectedly, protests in 2013 closed down the museum. Local people think the building is telling the story of a government that builds monuments but does not build houses. Looters have tried to take the buildings' materials and its contents. Authorities are trying to protect it, while the government responds to these tough questions. Places have lives of their own and different meanings evolve from those intended.

Narratives can be transformative. The goal of this book is to nudge major strands of narrative toward non-fiction. As with *Rashomon*, there are inevitably many strands. The authors like to think of an effective design narrative as creative non-fiction, a story that takes inspiration from factual information about how people use places. It is all too easy to slide into a single strand of narrative built largely on artistic vision and hope. In the words of Nigerian novelist Chimamanda Ngozi Adichie, "When we reject the single story, when we realize that there is never a single story about any place, we regain a kind of paradise."[15] Design demands creativity to include the facts, many of them awkward and ambiguous, which is the way with social life. Facts may not support a designer's original concept, but may push and pull a narrative, adding depth that creates a place more easily appreciated on more levels and by a more diverse population over time.

Notes

1 Karl Marx, *Das Kapital*, vol. 1, ch. 7, section 1, 1867. Quote retrieved August 24, 2016 at: https://en.wikiquote.org/wiki/Architecture.

2 Ebba Koch and Richard André Baraud, *The Complete Taj Mahal: And the Riverfront Gardens of Agra* (London: Thames & Hudson, 2006), 239.

3 "Plea to rewrite Taj history dismissed," *The Hindu*, July 14, 2000. Retrieved July 2, 2015 at: www.thehindu.com/thehindu/2000/07/14/stories/0214000q.html; "Taj Mahal part of an ancient temple: UP BJP chief," *The Hindu*, December 8, 2014. Retrieved July 2, 2015 at: www.thehindu.com/news/taj-mahal-part-of-an-ancient-temple-uttar-pradesh-bjp-chief/article6672772.ece.

4 Author Jenny Young's remembrances.

5 Maya Lin lecture, fall 2014, Eugene, Oregon.

6 This unpublished material was originally viewed confidentially. The design of destination resorts occurs within a highly competitive industry. The Christopher Grubbs illustrations shown here are available following construction of the resort.

7 Diller, Scofidio + Renfro. Blur Building. Swiss Expo 2002, Yverdon-les-Bains, Switzerland, 2002.

8 Russell Ellis and Dana Cuff, *Architects' People* (New York: Oxford University Press, 1989).

9 Le Corbusier, *The Modulor: A Harmonious Measure to the Human Scale, Universally Applicable to Architecture and Mechanics* (Basel & Boston: Birkhäuser 2004). First published in two volumes in 1954 and 1958.

10 Le Corbusier, *Vers une Architecture* (Paris: Éditions Vincent, Fréal, 1958).

11 Roger Griffith and Anne Grady, "Le Corbusier Kitchen Conservation: Video Update," *Inside/Out: A MoMA/MoMA PS1 Blog*, May 9, 2013. Retrieved August 24, 2016 at: www.moma.org/explore/inside_out/category/le-corbusier-kitchen-conservation/. One of the kitchens was reconstructed at the Museum of Modern Art in New York in 2012.

12 Nigel Coates, *Narrative Architecture*, Architectural Design Primer Series (Hoboken, NJ: Wiley, 2012).

13 Akira Kurosawa, *Rashomon*, Daia Film Company, 1950.

14 Karen Eicker, "Red Location Cultural Precinct," *Architectural Record*, August 2012. Retrieved August 23, 2016 at: Archrecord.construction.com/projects/portfolio/2012/08/Red-Location-Cultural-Precinct-Noero-Wolff-Architects.asp.

15 Chimamanda Ngozi Adichie, "The Danger of a Single Story," filmed July 2009 at TEDGlobal 2009.

Figure 2.1
High Line, New York City, James Corner, Field Operations, and Diller Scofidio + Renfro
Architects, Jenny Young, photographer

Chapter 2
Whose Place is This?

Whose woods these are I think I know.[1]

Robert Frost

Successful places typically reflect multiple viewpoints and diverse human experience. Responsive, equitable, interesting, handsome places commonly grow out of and reflect diverse visions, goals, skills, and responsibilities. Rarely does one individual own, design, or use a large place. Yet many own it at some point in the process.

Who Owns this Place?

Buildings embody the dreams, compromises, mandates, science, and politics of a diverse cast of characters. This complexity is evident in the story of Pruitt-Igoe,[2] a famous, failed, public project, thirty-three high-rise apartment blocks, in which after two decades no one wanted to live. Pictures from the early 1950s show well-dressed, happy children playing on the lawns and well-maintained living/dining rooms and bedrooms. Pictures from the early 1970s show garbage, broken windows, gangs, and children running wild. What happened? How did the community lose ownership of this place?

In the early 1950s the architect Minoru Yamasaki designed what he thought was successful housing.[3] The new residents were delighted when they moved in and remember Pruitt-Igoe as the first nice place they had ever lived, mentioning that it had plumbing that worked and views like a resort. Some still remember living in Pruitt-Igoe in the 1950s as the happiest time of their lives. Community get-togethers were common and positive. Civic leaders described this housing with pride as light and clean with all the modern conveniences. They owned the accomplishment of providing decent housing for St. Louis's working poor. Public housing administrators spoke of the quality of the housing. If people were asked at that time whose place it was, many would say it was theirs.

Fast-forward to the late 1960s. The economy in St. Louis had grown during World War II, but post-war industry declined, and contrary to expectations, the economy faltered. The inner city could support fewer workers and unemployment grew. At the same time, new suburbs were developed with white-only covenants, and the inner city became more segregated, as it lost population. Empty apartments began to appear in Pruitt-Igoe, as the more successful residents left. They became poorer and had more problems. The people who lived there were stigmatized. Pruitt-Igoe became a place for people who had no other options. They visited their anger on the buildings. Broken windows and urine-stained elevators became signature features. Crime made it a scary place. With rent coming in from only a fraction of the apartments, the housing authority could afford only minimal maintenance and provided little security. Community resources did not supplement this meager budget. Maintenance became worse and worse.[4]

Whose place was Pruitt-Igoe then? Only those with glowing memories from those early years would say it was their place. No one was taking charge. The thirty-three residential towers, which promised so much in 1954, were dramatically demolished two decades later. The first block was imploded on live television in 1972, and by 1976, Pruitt-Igoe became a rough, empty piece of land.

Why was this once-exemplary place not sustainable? Similar buildings worked well in Singapore and New York

City. The tragic story of Pruitt-Igoe has been told many times, and many have been blamed. It is an object lesson in the humble role of place, when politics, social welfare systems, segregation, employment, and other forces take a turn for the worse. There is no easy scapegoat for this failure.

Fortunately, many stories about making and maintaining places have happier endings. People, as did the early residents of Pruitt-Igoe, take satisfaction in claiming and occupying space. Unlike ants that have no boundaries with respect to each other, humans have territorial instincts. People choose environments or modify them to protect their backs and see what is coming. They root themselves, where they have refuge and prospect.

There is deep satisfaction in having one's own turf. Ownership, never absolute, constitutes a particular and definable bundle of rights, that have changed over time and remain different throughout the world. For thousands of years people have had territorial but not legal rights and roamed large portions of the globe. As people began to claim land for themselves, they identified their territory with layers of markers, from outpost towers to settlements with walls and gates to control access. Today, most of the habitable land in the world has legal property boundaries. With the exception of a small pie-shaped section of Antarctica, nations and within them individuals and groups own almost all the land on the planet. Ownership has been challenged within and among communities throughout human history. Battles have been fought over even very small places of unlikely value. Changes in ownership over time are complex.

A History of Many Owners

Take the example of Martha's Vineyard,[5] which like many places in the United States has had many owners. This island was formed by glaciers during the Ice Age. As the earth warmed and topography stabilized, birds brought seeds, and plants took hold. The first human residents, later known as Wampanoags, came by canoes from the mainland. They settled the whole island hunting and gathering without thinking of owning in a contemporary sense.

The first white settlers, who came many years later, brought a new concept of ownership. In 1602, Bartholomew Gosnold spotted Martha's Vineyard from his ship while searching for sassafras. He later claimed the islands for England. Thomas Mayhew purchased rights to the land. His son settled to teach Christianity to the local people. Others bought land and established towns. European diseases decimated the native peoples, and they retreated to Gay Head on the western end of the island. In recent times, they renamed this place Aquinnah, using an ancient name to reclaim their ancient ownership.

Whaling brought a black whaling captain, other free blacks, and Portuguese fishermen to settle permanently on Martha's Vineyard. As the whaling economy was dying, the tourist industry grew. Whaling captains' houses became hotels and homes for summer people. With the era of religious revivals, the island became a center for Methodists and later Baptists, who first came for a few weeks each summer, and later built more permanent houses. Cottage City, later renamed Oak Bluffs, became one of the first American summer resorts. Middle-class blacks came first for revival meetings and built summer homes too. More came with the Harlem Renaissance.

The people of Martha's Vineyard have had mixed loyalties. As an island, they remained loyal to Britain during the revolutionary war, but ultimately became part of the United States, first as part of Duke's County, New York, but later as part of Massachusetts. A secessionist flag featuring a white seagull can occasionally be seen.

Whose place is it? The population grows in the summer to 150,000 and shrinks to 15,000 in the winter. Martha's

Vineyard continues to be an interesting example of the melting pot that is America.[6]

Claiming Places

There have been disputes over territory on Martha's Vineyard, as there have been in most parts of the globe. Like other animals, humans identify their territory. Animals need territory for safety, for propagation, and for securing food. They claim territory through biologic mechanisms, such as urinating. Some animals make constructions as well, like the male bowerbirds of Australia, who build elaborate nests to attract mates. Similarly, for people, an important part of owning a place is protecting it and making it secure. Humans mark territory they control with a wide array of physical barriers and symbols. While these barriers and symbols have their roots in the need for shelter and security, they are also about self-expression and identity. The clothes people wear, the cars they buy, the houses they choose, and the ways they decorate their gardens and interiors are all ways they personalize space, expressing not just ownership, but who they are, to themselves and to other people.

The design of places can help people claim space to make their territory more secure. Architect and city planner Oscar Newman and others have studied how to make neighborhoods safer and coined the term "defensible space."[7] Defensible space is different from a world of fenced and gated communities, of indestructible walls that strive to prevent personalization and yet inspire vandalism, of spikes on a bench so a homeless person cannot transform it into a bed. Defensible space is not defensive, but rather offers a framework for people to control territory in ways that support community, while ensuring safety and reinforcing identity.

Ambiguity of ownership can create problems. In-between spaces, where it is hard to say who has agency, are often contested zones, where criminal activity can thrive. Safe design encourages people to know their neighbors and look out for them. Positioning doors and windows in a design to permit clear visibility of public areas results in natural surveillance of a friendly sort. Lighting helps, but only if there are others around to note criminal activity. Channeling foot traffic to common paths can create a friendly crowd that discourages irresponsible and criminal behavior. Well-maintained places signal that someone cares and will defend them. Places with broken windows and unkempt lawns suggest lack of effective ownership and invite territorial encroachment.

Newman's plans for an inner-city neighborhood and a low-cost housing project used a variety of means to increase people's sense of ownership and reduce crime rates. In neighborhood projects in Dayton, Ohio, and South Bronx, New York, under-used and under-supervised areas were assigned purposes and owners. Traffic patterns were changed in Dayton to serve local residents and divert through-traffic. Decorative gates were added to control access to nine new mini-neighborhoods. In New York, gathering places like playgrounds received added seating and lighting. Individual townhouses gained fenced front and back yards and were painted different colors. This combination of changes reduced apartment turnover and decreased the crime rate, building more stable communities.

Personalizing Places

One way people express both themselves and their ownership of places is by adding their own personal touches. Environmental psychologist Robert Sommer contrasts places that discourage personalization with places that welcome and support self-expression, terming them "hard" and "soft."[8] He asks questions like: Can chairs be moved in a classroom or a public square, or are they fixed? Places can suppress or encourage customization. Designers can have a love–hate relationship to the question of how their projects are decorated and furnished. Designers frequently take their own type of ownership of their projects, which can lead to conflicts when the designs become places for someone else to live.

At one end of the spectrum are architects famous for designing everything. Architect Ludwig Mies van der Rohe sought purity in the design of his landmark, closet-less Farnsworth House. He reportedly told Dr. Farnsworth, "You only need one dress. Hang it on the hook on the back of the bathroom door." He opened the walls with glass, bringing the landscape inside, but providing only modest wall space for artwork.[9] The effect was stunning and the building continues to be an architectural treasure. Sometimes treasures are hard to live with, and in fact, no one has truly lived for any length of time in the beautifully austere Farnsworth House. It is a work of art.

At the other end of the spectrum, some designers see their work as frameworks for people to take over and complete as they wish. Examples include architect John Habraken's concepts of support structures and infill[10] and Lucien Kroll's housing projects, including medical student housing at Leuven University in Belgium.[11] These projects provided the structural frameworks, within which individuals were able make their own choices about layout and finishes. The first tenants could make these choices, and over time the places have acquired more richness and variety.

Architect Herman Hertzberger's idea of "incompleteness"[12] offers another perspective. Hertzberger writes about designing buildings that bristle with intentional "imperfections" that can be interpreted in various ways and augmented to suit individual needs. For the elderly, he created a small, unassigned alcove at the entry to each tiny apartment, offering a place to display anything from Delft plates to potted plants. Residents could comfortably pull out a chair and venture shyly into the community with a cup of cocoa, much as one might on a front porch. In family housing front yards, Hertzberger left unfinished concrete block work, a sketchy construction that suggested the beginnings of a fence or porch railing. These rough elements were not decorative and actually seemed to demand a response. Householders responded in varied ways. The architecture provided an essential but not dogmatic nudge. People thus claimed ownership of their yards, making a first tentative step toward engaging with the neighborhood. Hertzberger uses the analogy of an instrument and the player. Form should provoke people into making choices most appropriate to their particular needs and desires.[13] Hertzberger writes,

> The more influence you can personally exert on the things around you, the more you feel emotionally involved with them, and the more attention you will pay to them, and also, the more you will be inclined to lavish care and love on the things around you.[14]

Levittown, an early American suburb, sold simple, basic, two-bedroom houses on bare lots. As families grew in size and wealth, they built a variety of additions and landscaping features, forming a varied and established neighborhood. In the Midwestern United States, in the 1950s it was common to see what were called basement houses. The first construction was a basement with a stair popping up out of it. Later on, when the family finances could manage, a house would appear on the basement foundation, and the family would move upstairs.

More recently, in Port Elizabeth, South Africa, Noero Wolff Architects experimented with building minimal basic houses on large lots, so owners themselves could add space over time.[15] In Iquique, Chile, architect Alejandro Aravena of the firm Elemental worked with such a small budget that only basic shells of 30 square meters (320 square feet) with roughed-out plumbing could be built. Residents moved in to personalize and transform the shells. Because each small house was planned next to an equal sized void, the residents were able to expand into the adjacent space over time.[16]

Multiple Actors, Multiple Viewpoints

When making places for people, every designer needs to ask whose place is this? As on Martha's Vineyard, every place has its own history, present and future. Designers need to take into account the breadth of ownership people feel as a community as well as the needs of particular clients and users.

For whom does a designer act? The most direct answer is the client. Clients hire designers when they want to modify their environments, making them larger or smaller or aspiring to a different feel or appearance. They may view space as a commodity to sell or lease. Whatever the motivation, a built project will be a significant investment of time and money. For smaller projects the owner may be an individual or a small group. For larger and more complex projects the client may be an enterprise or institution and may be represented by a professional project manager who can organize and control the process.

The owner has a big voice in the process. With economic responsibility the owner wants value for investment. Many owners entering the design process may think they are the only voice, but there are other voices. Designers are licensed by the state to protect the community.

The future users, the people who will actually occupy the place, may have a different stake than the owners and different needs. Take the example of a school project. The administrators want the project to be a safe place for teachers and students, with identity in the community. Custodians want the place to be easy to keep clean and repair. Teachers want indoor and outdoor classrooms that support a multifaceted educational approach flexibly, lots of storage, and good sound insulation from the next classroom. Children would like the classroom to be fun and not boring. The parents would like the place to be safe and welcoming for their children and provide a stimulating environment for physical, social, and intellectual learning. In multicultural communities, parents also want the school to support their home culture. This list is long.

The neighbors also have something to say about what a project looks like, how tall it is, what kind of sun shadow it casts, how close it is to the lot line, how many parking spaces it has, and so forth. Neighbors feel that they "own" the neighborhood, which plays out with political action, a practice known as NIMBYism (not in my back yard). Legal measures like building codes are often augmented by qualitative measures like design review. Maintaining community character and supporting the goals of residents involves ideas about what a good community looks like and how it works. As anyone who has been involved in building construction knows, regulation is a thicket of sometimes conflicting and confusing rules. In a contemporary, rapidly changing world some standards may be different from the owner's or designer's, but challenging these rules is indeed challenging, and can add years to a construction schedule. At times it seems that the building codes own the building.

Engineers represent the voice of building science. Contemporary efficient resource use and energy conservation practices affect gardening, paving, building orientation, fenestration, and pretty much everything else, including public relations in today's greening world. Banks are looking for reliable collateral before making a loan. Builders talk about "their" places. They own, if not the constructed place, the experience of building it.

Last, but not least, designers, although dedicated to providing a service to clients that integrates all these different goals, have their own goals. One way people make places their own is through their choice of designer. When clients look for a designer, they consider several factors: cost of services, personal compatibility, recommendations from trusted peers, and relevant professional experience. Careful clients review the designer's previous projects and visit them if possible. Selecting a particular designer is not neutral. It includes some predilection the client feels for the character of projects the designer makes and often reflects the kind of identity in the project the client seeks.

Not uncommonly, designers think of projects they design as their own, as in the example of the Farnsworth House. This feeling of ownership often contributes to an intense involvement with the building and donation of many hours of work to make sure the final product is done well.

More than that, designers often seek to position their designs in the largest possible context. How does this project advance the art of placemaking? How can this project be designed to provide what is needed now, but also what will be useful in the future? How can this project increase social equity in the community and in the world? How can this project sustain habitat for non-human species, as well? How can this project conserve resources and mitigate climate change? In the global world, people are just beginning to understand how many small decisions made locally can have far reaching global effects.

Participatory Design

Placemaking is a complex social process. Participatory design processes, which include the client, the potential users, and the future users in the design, have important roles in giving the designer accurate information and helping people achieve agency over place. For small projects, this process may be conversations between the designer and the client, a walk-through of the client's current place, discussions of what

Figure 2.2
Design Charrette, Eugene, Oregon, Kaarin Knudson, photographer

works and what doesn't work, a visit to some projects that
the client or designer identifies as having good ideas to
consider. For larger and more complex projects, participatory
processes include survey data collection, focus groups, design
workshops, open houses and presentations, and other means
of building consensus for decisions. This is time worth
spending. It is better than guessing, which generally leads to
multiple revisions, wasting time, and resources.

Participants in the design process may not be the people
who finally occupy the project. Over time the context changes
and needs change. Part of any participatory process should
consider the future. For example, not so many years ago
every project was focused on cable trays for Internet
connection to every workstation. Today Wi-Fi frees some
workstations from being fixed to one spot. Stewart Brand
proposes "scenario buffering," as a process to consider the
impact of future forces on any project. He argues, "All
buildings are predictions. All predictions are wrong."[17]

He encourages participants to outline the driving forces of the times, including shocking and unthinkable worst-case visions, and then to summarize a handful of possible scenarios against which to test the design. With this context, teams can design for future viability.

Unfortunately, some participatory processes may be aimed primarily at public relations or meeting legal requirements for participation. Essential stakeholders may not be invited. Workshops may be scheduled too late to integrate significant new ideas in the design. Participation can be so inconsistent that the same meeting is held over and over to include new participants. These efforts alienate people, who see their ideas ignored. Stakeholders may not show up the next time a call goes out for participation. Effective participation will not be supported if the neighborhood eccentric is the only participant.

Finally, Whose Place will this Be?

Most places outlive their first owners, their designers, and their original purposes. An average American homeowner stays in a house for ten to fifteen years. The building will likely long outlast its original tenants. Will a place retain its usefulness? Use too much energy? Meet future health and safety standards? Support individuals and groups, community and privacy? Does it have historic or artistic value? Has it become a treasured part of the urban fabric? Is it obsolete? Is it sensual? Beautiful? Should it be reused, renovated, or recycled?

The challenge is to invent built forms that retain value for continued ownership, meeting individual and community needs now and in the future. In the end, while one individual may provide creative leadership, successful places typically reflect multiple viewpoints and diverse human experience.

Notes

1   Robert Frost, "Stopping by Woods on a Snowy Evening," 1923.
2   Yamasaki & Associates: Minoru Yamasaki, Architect, Pruitt-Igoe, St. Louis, Missouri, 1954.
3   Minoru Yamasaki, the architect, designed similar housing in New York City that did not experience the problems of the Pruitt-Igoe housing.
4   Chad Freidrichs, *The Pruitt-Igoe Myth* (2012). The Pruitt-Igoe story is told in detail in this full-length documentary film available on YouTube. Retrieved August 24, 2016 at: www.youtube.com/watch?v=xKgZM8y3hso.
5   Paul Schneider, *The Enduring Shore: A History of Cape Cod, Martha's Vineyard and Nantucket* (New York: Henry Holt, 2000).
6   Historian David McCullough first introduced this idea to author Jenny Young.
7   Oscar Newman, *Creating Defensible Space* (Washington, DC: US Dept. of Housing and Urban Development, Office of Policy Development and Research, 1996), 31–79.
8   Robert Sommer, *Tight Spaces: Hard Architecture and How to Humanize It* (Upper Saddle River, NJ: Prentice Hall, 1974).
9   William Norwich, "Sex and Real Estate," *New York Times Magazine*, June 1, 2003.
10 N. John Habraken, J. T. Boekholt, and P. J. M. Dinjens, *Variations: The Systematic Design of Supports*, Laboratory of Architecture and Planning at MIT, 1976. Marc Schwarz, *De Drager* [Supports]: *A Film about Architect John Habraken*, schwarzpictures, 2012. Retrieved August 24, 2016 at: https://vimeo.com/61410893.
11 Lucien Kroll and Peter Blundell Jones, *The Architecture of Complexity* (Cambridge, MA: Massachusetts Institute of Technology, 1987).
12 Herman Hertzberger, *Lessons for Students in Architecture*, translated from the Dutch by Ina Rike (Rotterdam: Uitgeverij 010, 1991).
13 Herman Hertzberger, "Shaping the Environment," in *Architecture for People,* Ed. Byron Mikellides (New York: Holt, Rinehart & Winston, 1980), 38–40.
14 Hertzberger, *Lessons for Students in Architecture*, 170.
15 Noero Wolff Architects, Museum at Red Location, New Brighton Township, Port Elizabeth, South Africa, 2005.
16 Elemental, Architect Alejandro Aravena, Quinta Monroy Housing, Iquique, Chile, 2003, published in Andres Lepik and Barry Bergdoll, *Small Scale, Big Change: New Architectures of Social Engagement* (New York: Museum of Modern Art, 2010).
17 Stewart Brand, "The Scenario-Buffered Building," *How Buildings Learn: What Happens After they're Built* (New York: Viking, 1994).

Chapter 3
Where is this Place?

There is no there there.[1]
Gertrude Stein, speaking of Oakland, California

Too often cities, suburbs, streets, and buildings cannot be distinguished by where they are. All over the world there are commercial strip-lined highways, chain restaurants, and bland structures. Outside Vicenza in Italy, on the fringe of Eugene, Oregon, along highways in China and Chile, South Africa and England, Israel and Canada, Mexico and Sweden, places often look the same. "The geography of nowhere" is how social critic James Kunstler[2] describes this phenomenon. Or is it the geography of everywhere? If, as poet Irene Hsiao claims, "place is still a marker of identity,"[3] when everyplace looks the same, who are we?

Making Places

When anthropologist Margaret Mead traveled to a new place, the first thing she did was create a familiar milieu for her daughter Catherine with her quilt and toy. It did not matter where she was, whether on a ship or in a hut on a tropical island, she created a familiar place.[4] In more difficult situations, such as on the front during World War I, in the Theresienstadt concentration camp, or in refugee camps in

Figure 3.1 *(facing page)*
Croatia, Mei-Li Hsiao, photographer

Jordan, people have the remarkable ability and the defiance[5] to recreate a bit of garden or home, transforming where they are into places with some hope and meaning.

Places are deeply embedded in their cultural geography. Anthropologists, historians of vernacular settlements, journalists, and artists have documented how different peoples have adapted to live in the enormous range of habitats of the planet, even very tough ones. At the extreme of the Arctic, the Inuit have survived by building with materials at hand: with snow and ice for their winter homes, and sealskins and driftwood for their summer homes. At another extreme, Tuareg people in the Sahara Desert herd cattle and live in tents and also settle in houses constructed out of local earth. The adobe houses give shade during the day and provide flat roofs, cool places to sleep at night, when the interior has become too hot.

The meaning of space and place grows out of human experience. Theorists such as architect Christian Norberg-Schulz, geographer Yi-Fu Tuan, and archaeologist Salvatore Settis[6] hypothesize that places have an underlying structure particular to their location and cultural context. The geographic characteristics of climate, proximity to water, altitude and topography, and flora and fauna set the physical stage for patterns of living. Cultural practices evolve: common languages, shared belief systems and rituals, social practices, and ways of finding expression through the arts. Particular ways of using space have led to richly varied cultural building patterns. As new generations of inhabitants continue to modify their environments, places gain layers and depth of meaning. Design contributes to place making and not just space making.

Making places anchor people in the world. Humans draw security from knowing where they are and from familiarity with the world around them. Anchored, people can comprehend and be competent in the environment, rather than feel threatened. Over time people typically invest themselves in the places they inhabit. After disasters like Hurricane Katrina, people are resilient and committed to their places; they work to rebuild with ingenuity, inventiveness, and stubbornness. Even after the Chernobyl nuclear disaster, over a thousand people defied authorities and resettled in the heavily contaminated Exclusion Zone. Nobel laureate Svetlana Alexievich collected oral histories from many of these residents. In 2013, more than twenty-five years after the disaster, 130 residents, mostly women in their eighties, were still alive. The women who stayed said that "Those who left are worse off now. They are all dying of sadness . . . Motherland is Motherland. I will never leave." Relocation has its own problems of anxiety and depression. Officials and journalists who have studied Chernobyl have found that the "self-settlers" outlive their counterparts who relocated by up to ten years, evidence of the power of connections to home and personal agency.[7]

In today's world, people may occupy multiple places, and human experience of place is nuanced through travel and through media. As the world becomes more and more homogenized, people hunger for places that speak: a stirring landscape, a quality of built world, and open spaces that have meaning and intensify experience. This hunger has put tremendous pressure on places that are memorable and evocative.

Many World Heritage sites around the world are experiencing this pressure. Lijiang, in Yunnan, China, is an 800-year-old town that was largely reconstructed after an earthquake to preserve the rich culture and craft tradition of the Naxi, one of many non-Han minority groups in China. Living for a year in Lijiang with a Naxi family, community planner Chiao-Yen Yang learned that nearly all the structures in the central historic district had been rented or sold to enterprising Han business people, who were successfully providing services to tourists. Clearly, the dilemma between historic urban fabric and traditional culture is hard to solve in a way that benefits everyone. Lijiang had been preserved as a beautiful stage-set, with the real human culture removed—in other words, Naxi space for people to consume, but not a Naxi place.[8]

Migrations

Cultures are not static. Today, few cultures are isolated from contact with others. Few people stay put. Humans are an adaptable and mobile species with a history of migrations that have been studied (and disputed) for years. Better opportunities pull people. Political and social pressures and intolerable conditions push others. Today, global communications, accessible travel, war, and disasters continue to result in human migrations. The World Bank estimated that in 2010 more than 215 million people, about 3 percent of the world's population, lived outside their countries of birth.[9] The current migration of Syrian refugees is one of many such diasporas that challenge human empathy, generosity, and ingenuity. The Jewish Diaspora, the exodus of Vietnamese boat people, the African Diaspora, and the partition of India into India and Pakistan all carried large numbers of people into a world not prepared to welcome them graciously.

People bring their culture with them when they migrate, but in new contexts, patterns and meanings change. It is not just that cultures change, but also how rapidly that change occurs. In the United States everyone is a migrant, some more recent than others. Minnesota today, for example, has 65,000 Hmong residents, a majority of whom live in St. Paul, making it the largest Hmong city in the world. The Hmong, the general population, and the place are all changing as a consequence.

Statistics about migrants do not include seasonal and voluntary migration. Margaret Mead was a voluntary migrant; a new place was an academic challenge and

Figure 3.2
Are These Women Celebrating Hmong New Year in Luang Prabang, Laos or St. Paul,
Minnesota? Noelle E. Jones, photographer

opportunity. For a privileged few, a seasonal migration to a lake cabin, a tropical beach, or a mountain lodge adds meaning and richness to their lives. For less privileged agricultural workers, journeying to where the crops are ripening places puts them and their families at the risk of homelessness.

Today, one of the largest migrations is the movement of rural people to cities. When immigrants arrive in cities, they settle wherever they can, often in places difficult to inhabit, where friends or family have gone before. In the United States, numerous urban ethnic neighborhoods emerged with earlier migrations: Cabbagetown, Finntown, Andersonville, Little Italy, Chinatown, Japantown. Some of these ethnic enclaves still exist, though often the immigrants no longer live there. New urban villages have appeared: little Kabul,

Figure 3.3
Whitechapel Neighborhood, London, Howard Davis, photographer

little Ethiopia, Bangladeshi-town. Each is distinctive and include local businesses that offer services desired by new immigrants. The diminutive "little" that often attaches to a neighborhood signals both the secondary status of the migrants and respect for the homeland.

Geographer and international development practitioner Nga Dao writes of the difficulties faced by Vietnamese mountain people who have been displaced by large reservoir and dam construction. Unlike American hydroelectric projects in wilderness areas, one Vietnamese project may displace many communities, most with minority populations. Relocated populations find it hard to move from a culture of subsistence farming and fishing to a contemporary global culture that does not value their previous skills. Government agencies and NGOs have struggled to find effective compensation for lost homes, jobs, and cultural landmarks.

Squatter settlements have developed worldwide from a lack of more desirable options in the short term, but once people are fixed in a spot, they make places. Investigative journalist Katherine Boo writes feelingly in her non-fiction narrative of the life in Annawadi, a now-demolished squatter settlement near the Mumbai airport and its luxury hotels.[10] Boo describes with personal detail how the impoverished earn a few rupees collecting and recycling garbage, and selling themselves if necessary. Even with horrible conditions that support crime and ill health, squatter life in the city may include hope where village life did not.

Some Peruvian squatter settlements, *barriadas*, grew out of collaborative initiatives rather than forced migrations and have become respectable suburbs of Lima. The civil engineers and architects participating in the original invasion of private land laid out logical street patterns and widths and marked off regular plots of land, laying the groundwork (literally) for ordered urban development. Many other squatter settlements have struggled with infrastructure issues, crime, disease, and conflicts over land ownership.

Hybrid Places

Taiwanese technology migrants illustrate how building cultures can be mixed. One group lives and works in two "Silicon Valleys"—Hsinchu, Taiwan, and Silicon Valley, California. These citizens of the world have two passports, degrees in both countries, speak two languages, and often own two houses, one Taiwanese and one Californian. Environmental design professor Shenglin Elijah Chang found that in California, these migrants emulated Taiwan and included features common to Taiwan. such as Japanese-style tatami rooms. In Taiwan, they emulated a California suburb with detached houses, lawns, and barbecues. These resourceful global technologists felt at home in two places, while longing for the place in which they were not.[11]

How does this change the way designers should think about contextual design, which has long added meaning to gardens, interiors, buildings, and urban places? In the context of migrations and global interconnections through travel and media, how do people understand the emerging world? Is it a melting pot or a mosaic? The image of the melting pot suggests that diverse flavors are blended together to form a new mix. The mosaic conjures a world made up of individual pieces, each crisp and strong, existing side by side in various combinations to make larger wholes. People seem to enjoy the differentness of different places. At the same time, people thrive and placemaking is inspired by new and sometimes unexpected influences.

The "slow cities" movement has the goal of maintaining place identity in this rapidly changing world. Its roots grew out of the slow food movement, which began as a battle to prevent a McDonald's from opening in Rome. Resisting the global hegemony and homogenization of fast food, locavore restaurants around the world stress a cuisine based on local foods and traditional methods. Slow cities follow a parallel approach.[12] Their organizations promote walkable, mixed-use cities with local identity and diversity. Worldwide members include Berwick-upon-Tweed, Great Britain; Göynük, Turkey; Jeonju, South Korea; Levanger, Norway; and Sebastopol, California. These are not big cities but towns which have significant historic centers intact. These towns aspire to be great places to live, which can grow and change, while retaining their inherent structure and character. Other organizations like the Congress of New Urbanism have studied successful historic centers to glean principles for contemporary urban development.[13] Critiques of this work point to the challenge of executing these urban design initiatives with diversity and richness.

In design and planning, eclectic approaches are common. They include the "remuddles" that Alice Carey, a historic preservation architect with a sense of humor, took great delight in photographing—for example, a glorious Victorian structure covered with the latest in brick-patterned, asphalt roll roofing. This happens in cookery as well, where fusion restaurants are wonderfully creative, but sometimes not wonderful. Many have experienced the rise of a kind of restaurant that American humorist Calvin Trillin has dubbed "Maison de la Casa House."[14] Yet architectural fusion can create wonderful places. The history of design is the history of fusion. Exposure to different kinds of beauty from different places inspires designers in all the arts, and environmental design is no exception.

Shanghai new towns offer an interesting example in the context of China's rapid urbanization. To accommodate millions of people moving to Shanghai from rural areas, the "One City, Nine Towns Development Plan" is establishing nine new city centers linked by rapid transit, while retaining green space and agricultural land. Each new town has been planned with a distinctive identity. Historically, French, British, and American concessions formed distinct parts of cosmopolitan Shanghai. In this vein, new town models include a Spanish town, an Italian town complete with canals, a German town, a Dutch town, a Scandinavian town, and a British town with pubs, of course. Reached by commuter trains, these evocative centers bring tourists, wedding photographers, and home buyers for the pleasant new residential neighborhoods.[15]

New towns, historically, find it difficult to develop the rich social life of traditional urban areas. This takes time. As they mature, these new Shanghai towns will present opportunities to learn about the effects of transplanting community design, landscapes, and buildings from halfway around the globe.

Site Repair

Historically, settlements developed at crossroads and in places where essential resources of water, food, and building materials were available. Towns developed at distances from each other, where each could be the market center for surrounding agricultural settlements and a refuge for travelers. Minnesota has many small counties to permit access within one day's travel to the county seat, even in heavy snow without motorized transport.

Choosing where to build today involves a different constellation of concerns. In the context of sprawling cities, people are recognizing that urban development should not overwhelm land needed for agriculture, recreation, wildlife, and wilderness. Portland, Oregon's urban growth boundary has become a model that protects open space and farmland from urbanization.[16] Pursued diligently, growth boundaries lead to redevelopment within urban zones and retain open space.

Urban redevelopment in urban zones has a very mixed history. When it involves tearing down existing neighborhoods, it can have tremendous social costs. Herbert

Gans chronicled the grief and despair of the people living in the West End of Boston when they were forced out by redevelopment,[17] not unlike the descriptions from Chernobyl. In other situations where not a neighborhood but a contaminated and disused industrial brownfield site is redeveloped, a useful and beautiful place can repair a toxic gap in the urban fabric.

New York's High Line[18] was created from an abandoned elevated train line that was a closed-off, unattractive hazard. The new High Line is a linear park that connects the neighborhoods along its length. People sit, chat, and stroll along its path, above the melee of the city's bustle, noise, and fumes. Beloved by locals and tourists, it has become a major economic generator in an undervalued part of the city.

The "Site Repair"[19] pattern in *A Pattern Language* argues for retaining the strong features of a place as part of a design and doing new construction on its troubled parts. Like an Asian martial art, this approach uses the power of a place, rather than opposing it, preserving what is most beautiful and functional. Most sites have strengths to build on, and most budgets lack the resources to remake everything. In social terms, this means preserving the strength of communities and neighborhoods. Geographic information systems (GIS) provide new tools for cataloging and evaluating community strengths and weaknesses.[20]

Location is particularly an issue for low-budget social service projects. Funding is limited and the need is enormous. Buildable prime sites with good transit are expensive. A sober-living program seeking a site will find that few neighborhoods welcome this use. Many program residents will have lost their drivers' licenses or cars and need public transportation. In Portland, Oregon, a community nonprofit, after a long search, found an old hotel downtown on Skid Row. There were problems: liquor was available at every street corner; the local population was not known for temperance of any sort; crime was common and worrisome.

However, rapid transit was excellent. Tenants would be able to get to their recovery programs and their jobs. The price was right. Few other buyers were interested in this location. With not many other choices, the organization decided to make this work. They renovated the old structure and brought it back to life as a respectable apartment building. Recovering individuals with chemical-dependency histories helped make it happen. The building looked great, but the nonprofit did not stop there. They took on the neighborhood, sending their residents to patrol the area, contributing sober eyes on the street and picking up trash. Others joined their walks. The streets became friendlier. They were so successful in making the neighborhood safe that they contributed both to the neighborhood's gentrification and to the recovery of the residents of the clean and sober housing. The area became so desirable that, when the institution wanted to expand, it could not afford adjacent properties. Interestingly, in ensuing years, neighborhoods are finding sober-living apartments more acceptable because the residents can be such responsible community members.[21]

In another part of Portland, across the river and far from downtown, wide connector streets separate odd bits of overlooked residential neighborhoods, where many of the city's immigrants find places to live. In this non-descript context, local community members came together with designers to propose Portland Mercado as an economic development project. The Mercado is both an incubator for new businesses and a public market, a hub of Latino culture.[22] Designed using a participatory process and taking more than eight years to realize, the Mercado transformed a dilapidated car lot into a lively community center with the leanest of budgets. Vibrant colors give it spirit. The incubator spaces are occupied. Food carts pull up to the picnic shelter. Where there was little meaningful context, there is now a nascent center. The Mercado is a seed, a first step in making a neighborhood better.

Figure 3.4
Portland Mercado Site Plan, Portland, Oregon, Scott Edwards Architecture

Figure 3.5
Portland Mercado View, Scott Edwards Architecture photograph

Portland Mercado, Portland clean and sober residence, and the High Line are examples of how to make a place matter, make it whole, and make it better. People and design ideas are migrating, adding challenging complexity to making places based on broad and deep understandings about the characteristics of what a place was, is, and can be. Designers need to ask themselves: should I design as if this new place could be anywhere in the world? How do I take inspiration from its context? How do I balance global and local? Observing what is good in a place, as well as its problems; listening to people who live and work there; and designing creatively to add broadly without subtracting existing amenity make a challenging brief for the designer—complex, rewarding, and requiring perseverance and commitment.

Notes

1   Gertrude Stein, *Everybody's Autobiography* (New York: Random House, 1937), 289.

2   James Howard Kunstler, *The Geography of Nowhere: The Rise and Decline of America's Man-Made Landscape* (New York: Simon & Schuster, 1993).

3   Irene Hsiao, *San Francisco Weekly*, July 22, 2014.

4   Mary Catherine Bateson, *With a Daughter's Eye: A Memoir of Margaret Mead and Gregory Bateson* (New York: W. Morrow, 1984).

5   Kenneth Helphand, *Defiant Gardens: Making Gardens in Wartime* (San Antonio, TX: Trinity University Press, 2006).

6   Christian Norberg-Schulz, *Genius Loci: Toward a Phenomenology of Space* (New York: Rizzoli, 1979). Yi-Fu Tuan, *Space and Place: The Perspective of Experience*, 5th ed. (Minneapolis, MN: University of Minnesota Press, 2001). Salvatore Settis, *Se Venezia Muore* (Turin, Italy: Einaudi, 2014).

7   Holly Morris, "After Chernobyl, they refused to leave," CNN, 8:48 pm ET, Thursday, November 7, 2013. Retrieved August 24, 2016 at: www.cnn.com/2013/11/07/opinion/morris-ted-chernobyl; Svetlana Alexievich, *Voices from Chernobyl: The Oral History of a Nuclear Disaster*, translated by Keith Gessen (New York: Picador, 2005).

8   Chiao-Yen Yang in conversation with author Christie Johnson Coffin (Chiao-Yen Yang, *Cultural Resilience in Asia: A Comparative Study of Heritage Conservation in Lijiang and Bagan*, Ph.D. thesis, University of Washington, 2014).

9   World Bank, *Migration and Remittances Factbook 2011*, 2nd ed. (Washington, DC: World Bank, 2010). Compiled by Dilip Ratha, Sanket Mohapatra, and Ani Siwal of the Development Prospects Group.

10 Katherine Boo, *Behind the Beautiful Forevers: Life, Death, and Hope in a Mumbai Undercity* (New York: Random House, 2012).

11 Shenglin Elijah Chang, *The Global Silicon Valley Home: Lives and Landscapes within Taiwanese-American Trans-Pacific Culture* (Palo Alto, CA: Stanford University Press, 2006).

12 The slow cities organization website: www.cittaslow.org.

13 Congress of New Urbanism and Emily Talen, *Charter of the New Urbanism*, 2nd ed. (New York: McGraw Hill, 2013.). Website: www.cnu.org.

14 Trillin, Calvin, *The Tummy Trilogy* (New York: Farrar, Straus and Giroux, 1994).

15 Harry Den Hartog, "Shanghai New Towns: Searching for Community and Identity in a Sprawling Metropolis," 4th International Conference of the International Forum on Urbanism (Delft, Netherlands, 2009).

16 Passed by the state legislature in the early 1970s under the leadership of Governor Tom McCall, the law requires every city and metropolitan area in the state to determine "a land use planning line to control urban expansion onto farm and forest lands."

17 Herbert Gans, *The Urban Villagers: Group and Class in the Life of Italian-Americans* (New York: Free Press of Glencoe, 1962).

18 James Corner Field Operations with Diller, Scofidio + Renfro, The High Line, New York, NY, 2003.

19 Christopher Alexander, Sara Ishikawa, Murray Silverstein et al. "Site Repair," *A Pattern Language* (New York: Oxford University Press, 1977), 508–512.

20 *New York Times* "Mapping the US Census," retrieved August 24, 2016 at: http://projects.nytimes.com/census/2010/map; "Mapping Poverty in America," retrieved August 24, 2016 at: www.nytimes.com/newsgraphics/2014/01/05/poverty-map; Robert Wood Johnson Foundation, "#CloseHealthGaps," produced by the Virginia Commonwealth University Center of Society and Health, retrieved August 24, 2016 at: www.rwjf.org/en/library/infographics/life-expectancy-maps.html; Social Explorer (Oxford University Press, 2010, www.socialexplorer.com) is a website that allows people to make their own maps based on United States census data for over 220 years.

21 Friedner Wittman, chemical dependency researcher and writer, in private conversation with author Christie J. Coffin, 1994

22 Scott Edwards Architecture, Project Architects: Lisa McClellan and Roseva Saa, Architects, Portland Mercado, Portland, Oregon, 2015.

Chapter 4
How Big is this Place?

There is a rash of studies underway designed to uncover the bad consequences of overcrowding. This is all very well as far as it goes, but it only goes in one direction. What about undercrowding? The researchers would be a lot more objective if they paid as much attention to the possible effects on people of relative isolation and lack of propinquity. Maybe some of those rats they study get lonely too.[1]

William H. Whyte

Size is one of the major features of any design. What makes a place the right size? Both crowded and underpopulated spaces occur in most environments. People are very clever at using places and can make even seriously undersized or oversized places work, usually at a price. Common metrics for determining a place's size include human dimensions, culture, functional needs, legal codes and standards, benchmark examples and prototypes, projected future growth, and budget. The diverse metrics employed to determine the right size seldom yield one simple answer. How big should a place be? Or should we ask in light of contemporary striving for carbon neutrality and resource conservation, how small should a place be? Can a design achieve its goals gracefully and functionally with less construction?

Figure 4.1 *(facing page)*
Peggy Guggenheim Museum Courtyard, Venice, Italy, Donald Corner, photographer

Too Big or Too Small?

Spaciousness is a key goal for most design projects. The size of a place adds prestige and gravitas. In the last several decades, American waistlines, buildings, and public places have all gained in size. Too much space can be luxurious and a source of opportunity, but it can also be lonely, wasteful, hard to supervise, and more costly. Building too big can result in empty places that use resources without providing appropriate value.

Can a place be too small? People in crowded places can have serious problems. Evidence has piled up on the side of the evils of crowding. The notorious Black Hole of Calcutta packed 146 people into a 4.3-meter by 5.5-meter (14-foot by 18-foot) dungeon space intended for fewer. Suffocation, heat stroke, and trampling contributed to fatality.[2] The Black Hole was definitely too small.

Beyond a size that creates obvious physical harm, it becomes harder to identify a reasonable minimum for size. Over time, minimum space allocations per person have been negotiated. Minimums have tended to rise with prosperity. Standards have changed since the days of log cabin homesteading and New York tenements, whose small size and high human density were criticized for the spread of infectious disease, the lack of amenity and privacy, inappropriate mixing of the sexes, and exposure to people with anger management and other behavioral health problems. Modern adventure travelers recount stories of enjoying minimal and overcrowded accommodations but seldom make this a permanent style of life.

American homes have grown in size even as families have become smaller. After World War II, many purchased modest homes that were less than 93 square meters [1000 square feet]. From 1970 to 2010 new home size grew from 111 to 222 square meters [1200 to 2400 square feet], while family size shrank from 3.5 to 2.6 individuals.[3] At this scale, each

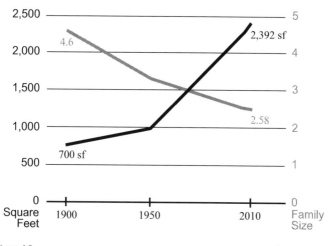

Figure 4.2
Graph Comparing Increasing House Size And Decreasing Family Size, US Census,

household member has approximately the same space as an American public school classroom.

Some aspire to even larger homes, which offer more prestige, privacy, and space for entertainment, homework, home businesses, and storage. Large places can offer more flexibility for harboring friends and relatives. A colleague expanded her house when her children left for college. It seemed odd at the time, but several years later her son returned to live at home with a new wife. Now there are two grandchildren, and the larger house has provided the elasticity to live as a multigenerational family. On the other hand, large houses use more energy, increase maintenance costs, and require larger mortgages. Investing in a large place can affect family resilience in times of financial slowdown and limit funds available for education, health care, retirement, and recreation.

At an urban scale, public spaces are often oversized and under-enclosed. William Whyte's study of public space in

New York concluded that successful places are often smaller than might be expected.[4] For a sense of community, a little bit of crowding is better than wide-open emptiness. There are exceptions, of course. The public squares of St. Peter's Basilica in Rome and Tiananmen Square in Beijing hold hundreds of thousands of people—not comfortable places for small groups, but an appropriate scale for large ceremonial gatherings.

A day spent walking through almost any American neighborhood will disclose underused spaces. Commercial space on the ground floor, often required for affordable housing, sometimes lacks an effective business plan and stays vacant for years. Detroit is the worst case, a city whose population has shrunk to less than half. Previously vibrant neighborhoods in Detroit have become zombie neighborhoods, suffering from the presence of empty, unmaintained structures.

Another source of empty dwellings in some neighborhoods is the second and third home phenomenon. The graceful, historic center of Charleston, South Carolina, has become a neighborhood of third homes for the wealthy, dark at night except during opera season. The value of real estate for an investment portfolio sometimes takes precedence over its value to the community. There are examples in rent-controlled communities where tenants use their low-cost apartments as second homes after they have moved elsewhere. Ironically, there are many homeless and others who search without success for affordable housing in the midst of underused real estate.

Human Size and Culture

Design starts with the size of the human body and interpersonal space. Human size and shape vary widely. Anthropometric and ergonomic research, now more sophisticated and more inclusive in documenting the range and details of human dimensions, is useful for designers.[5] Industrial designers carefully consider detailed human measurements, like finger size and rotational flexibility in designing objects like the iPhone. For something like counter heights, dimensions can be adjusted to the actual people who will be using them. A custom counter in basketball player Stephen Curry's kitchen might be different from one in World Champion gymnast Simone Biles' kitchen. In Head Start facilities, child-sized toilets and lavatories help children develop autonomy by acquiring basic hygiene skills. Landscape, building, and room dimensions may be commonly based on average sizes, even though no one person is average.

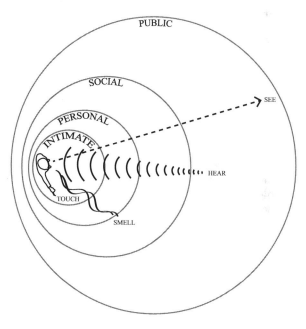

Figure 4.3
Personal Space Diagram, based on Edward T. Hall, Amanda Hansen, illustrator

Critical to sizing places is understanding the appropriate spacing among people. People regulate their contact with each other and structure their built worlds in part by maintaining body privacy through distance. For one-to-one conversations, people are comfortable in a personal zone. For larger groups, a social zone provides greater interpersonal distances among individuals. In public situations, visible people speaking loudly and persuasively can capture the attention of others even though they may be up to 8 meters [25 feet] away. Anthropologist Edward T. Hall helped State Department diplomats learn comfortable distances for social interaction when stationed abroad. He identified appropriate distances, which vary from culture to culture. His studies indicated, for example, that Arabs preferred a very close personal distance that made Americans feel crowded.[6]

The Japanese traditionally live in small places with paper walls and are said to have evolved ways to ignore activity that they can see, hear, and even smell, if that activity deserves privacy. Big city residents in Manhattan and San Francisco often live in very much smaller residences than suburbanites, because small is affordable. When houses are small and crowded, people do some of their living outside on the stoops and in neighborhood cafés, libraries, and parks. A contemporary urbanite uses the city to expand personal space. Urbanites might go to the corner coffee shop to write in peace, surrounded by others all hard at work on their laptops. Ironically, even though houses may be larger in the suburbs, suburbanites, too, are choosing to work in these places, but in this case for the companionship and community, not because they need the space.

Finding the Right Size

Creating a new place usually begins by itemizing the reasons for the new accommodations. This starts with people and their activities. Who is doing what with whom? For example, designing an alcove space off a living room might begin with figuring out how much space two people need to talk together in easy chairs.

As places increase in complexity, owners and/or design teams develop detailed narratives that outline goals and create functional programs for space. To calculate a building size, each desired and necessary space is identified and sized, based on who is doing what with whom. A factor is added for circulation and building systems.[7] Rules can determine size, like the dimensions of sports fields and tennis courts. Building codes and guidelines also provide some limits on size, usually minimums. Some specific uses are regulated in detail; for example, under common codes in the United States a bedroom may not be smaller than 70 square feet (6.5 square meters) and requires a closet. These requirements are based on negotiated standards and are not always logical for a particular case.

Size is one of the variables that people can learn from prototypical buildings and institutional assumptions and standards. Experiencing space by being there and observing how activities happen gives information to adjust sizes, as well as providing insight into other spatial qualities. People have different spatial yardsticks that they use as measurements. A measure called a *ping* works in Taiwan as an easy-to-remember metric, equivalent to two tatami mats or about 3.3 square meters (35 square feet). Taiwanese know the meaning of a 6-ping space; that is the professor's office.

Both an advantage and a pitfall of functional space programming is thinking of each function individually and identifying its need for a space. A thorough, thoughtful functional program can result in a large, lightly populated place. Although some of these needs may be overlaid on each other to achieve economies, the time and energy to negotiate shared arrangements may be outside the scope for either a building committee or a design team. In reality, most spaces can and do serve different functions over the day, week, or year. Of course, there are exceptions: some medical care spaces should be vacant, clean, and fully equipped to serve emergency patients.

Some spaces are seldom used. Consider the office meeting room for the monthly or weekly all-staff meeting. For the cost of heating, cooling, cleaning, repairing, and building a large meeting room, other solutions might be available. Investing in a good meal for the staff in a local restaurant banqueting room is surely cheaper and possibly more fun. If that violates expense accounting rules, sharing with other departments can often work by coordinating schedules. Unfortunately, shared space requires management time, which may not be available on anyone's busy schedule.

Another question is which spaces can be combined or eliminated? Imaginative schools use other community spaces to expand their horizons. A Californian summer day camp in Berkeley works out of a synagogue, and every day the children take long walks to use parks and other available community places. Perspectives Charter School[8] was built in downtown Chicago on an odd, triangular site. Because the site was so small, the school arranged for students to use a nearby gym and local theater, furthering the school's mission to connect students with the community in their daily lives.

Many schools benefit from thinking this way, because public schools are often planned very tightly. Californian elementary schools provide a median overall area of 6.8 square meters (73 square feet) per pupil,[9] compared with office planning which may commonly allocate a net usable area of between 14 and 20 square meters (150 to 215 square feet) per office worker.[10] School districts argue that they achieve economies of space by building fewer larger schools, leaving old neighborhood schools across town empty. This trend has social consequences, however. Neighborhood schools play important roles in their communities, and people battle to keep them open.

Most functional programs estimate future growth and change. A common practice is to add space for future needs. Planners use a variety of methods to project for growth but seldom consider what happens if needs get smaller. For example, since Internet banking and the credit card economy have reduced the need for space for face-to-face contact, local banks have ended up oversized. When the excitement of design is in the air, it is easier to plan for growth than for shrinkage or delay.

Size and Budget

Size (square meters or square feet) is the primary multiplier for cost in planning projects. Early in the design process, every project needs to balance size with budget. The problem is that budget and actual need for facilities are often not aligned. A close analysis of actual need frequently requires painful adjustments reducing size or quality of work to meet a budget.

Calculating size based on cost seems easy: simply divide the available funding by the dollars per square meter (square feet) of construction of the desired quality; basic arithmetic reveals the size one can afford. In performing budget calculations, it is important to make sure that all the costs outside of construction costs (the general contractor's contract) are included.[11] These additional project costs can range from 20 percent to 60 percent of the construction costs. The confusion between construction costs and the often much higher completed project costs can fuel unnecessary confusion and criticism, even newspaper headlines.

Changing Standards

Convention also affects size. It is rare that time is available to rethink everything, and modeling new construction on existing built forms is unavoidable. Large businesses, like national chain stores and restaurants, and large institutions, like the Department of Veterans Affairs, develop carefully worked-out templates of layout, space sizes, and character of finishes to direct all their construction projects. Because times change and ideas become outmoded, successful enterprises have processes to make detailed positive improvements based on new experience and new trends.

The Department of Veterans Affairs, for example, has a meticulous set of standards that represents their particular culture of medical space use. On their website anyone can find specific requirements they have formulated for almost every type of space.[12] These standards tend to err on the side of generosity. Their templates direct designers to include a high proportion of private offices in making a program for a new building. Lately, however, the VA has been experimenting with a culture change, adopting what is called "lean design." This approach tries to systematically eliminate waste in both process and space in order to increase productivity.[13] The VA Lean initiative is planning an open bullpen with small desks for health-care professionals rather than private offices. As a physician once said, "I mainly use my office to store my gym shoes." A lockable file drawer in a desk could accommodate her shoes. The new approach aims to increase interdisciplinary consultation as well as to save space. There are concerns, however, that physician recruitment could be negatively affected as a private office signals status.

Another example from hospital design points out how ideas about what is the right size change over time. In the nineteenth century, Florence Nightingale revolutionized hospital architecture by promoting compact open wards with twenty-four to thirty-six patients. The Nightingale ward, a long room lined with beds and tall windows on both sides for light and cross-ventilation, ushered in a more wholesome,

Figure 4.4
Nightingale Ward, Hampstead Smallpox Hospital, United Kingdom, World History Archive

daylighted, and naturally ventilated hospital environment. Reports from one of the last operational Nightingale wards in the United States stress how staff can see patients at a glance and patients have options for companionship during long convalescences.[14]

In the twenty-first century, the new standard for American hospitals mandates all single bedrooms for some very good reasons. Today, long convalescences seldom occur in the hospital. Patients are usually sicker, and family and friends who come to support the patient appreciate the privacy. Infection control is improved by separating patients. There are fewer medical mishaps where one patient is confused with another. Returning to the more crowded standard for health care is not an option, but there are consequences. New nursing floors have huge footprints, six or more times the size of Nightingale wards per bed. Staff complain of the distances walked daily, adding eight kilometers (five miles) per day or more. This exercise may

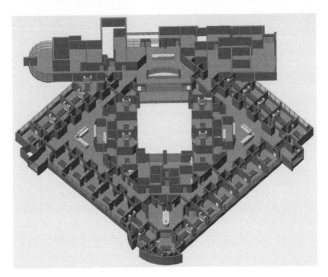

Figure 4.5
Twenty-First-Century Acute Care Wing, Axonometric Plan, The Design Partnership, architects

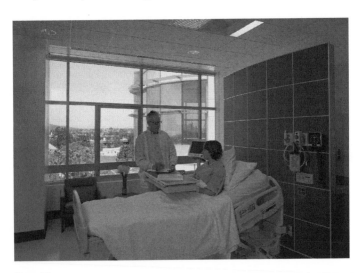

Figure 4.6
Twenty-First-Century Acute Care Patient Room, The Design Partnership, architects,
John Linden, photographer

contribute to staff fitness, but an eight-kilometer walk consumes about 20 percent of an eight-hour work shift.[15] When staff are spread out in a larger area, close-by support may be harder to find. Casual contact and cooperation may be less frequent and may handicap collaboration, sense of community, and medical response time.

Worldwide resources and standards differ widely. While the standard American hospital may be sized for single rooms and large professional staffs, an African hospital, like the Butaro Hospital in Rwanda, is sized like a Nightingale ward with an open, naturally ventilated room for multiple beds and provides excellent care with more limited resources.[16] Interestingly, the designers turned the Nightingale ward plan inside out. The beds face out to the windows, and a low, shared, service wall, consolidating expensive technology, is behind them. Everyone is visible to staff, and the patients have views and a bit more privacy.

Challenges to conventional sizing and building codes include the micro-apartment movement. Recently, developer Patrick Kennedy has been building apartments that are under 28 square meters (300 square feet) in the San Francisco area, inspired by both a 7-square-meter (78-square-foot) airstream trailer and a local shortage of rental property. Kennedy's proposal for homeless housing is even smaller at 15 square meters (160 square feet), which is similar to many single-room occupancy hotels (SROs).[17] Single renters and students, who are sick of sharing with deadbeat housemates, welcome this controversial development.

Micro-apartments have been criticized for not meeting typical community standards, but research on single-room occupancy housing in San Francisco reported that space was not the most cited concern. Residents felt their very tiny rooms had enough space. They sought improvement to basic utilities, ventilation and acoustic separation.[18]

The United States General Services Administration (GSA) has learned a lot recently about reduction of space. For staff

Figure 4.7
Micro-Apartment Interior, Patrick Kennedy, developer, Keith Baker, photographer

who spend much of their time in the field, the GSA has dropped space standards significantly, up to 50 percent. They are in the process of implementing this change. Taxpayers have already saved, as some leaseholds have been discontinued, and the population of others has dramatically increased—even doubled. The significant questions still to be answered are whether the reduction in space promotes quality work, efficiency, and employee satisfaction. Are workers prospering in smaller space?

There are clever ways to make space more productive and reduce overall size. A fold-up bed in the family bedroom or guestroom frees space for other study or recreation. Using shelving and cabinets to define office workspaces can double the usage of circulation aisles and locate storage closer to point of use. Making space more versatile does incur its own costs for purchasing, installing, and maintaining space-saving elements.

Along with a raft of challenging discussions and negotiations to reduce space use, a smaller building generally means smaller fees and prestige, not larger, for designers, contractors, managers, and landlords. Designers and builders are often rated by their abilities to deliver at a low cost per square meter (or square foot), and compact, densely developed space is more expensive. These perverse incentives make size a sustainability nut that is hard to crack. Yet building to an optimum size can have many benefits: lower overall construction costs, reduced energy use, space to achieve goals with compactness that facilitates communication and collaboration, space for future growth and change, and more affordable costs for building maintenance. How small can this place be?

Notes

1   William H. Whyte, www.pps.org/reference/wwhyte.
2   Commonly reported in histories of India, although the particular numbers are disputed.
3   *State of the Nation's Housing 2015*, Joint Center for Housing Studies of Harvard University, 2015.
4   William H. Whyte, *The Social Life of Small Urban Spaces* (New York: Project for Public Spaces, 1980). Retrieved August 25, 2016 at: www.pps.org/reference/wwhyte
5   Alvin R. Tilley and Henry Dreyfuss Associates, *The Measure of Man and Woman: Human Factors in Design*, rev. ed. (Hoboken, NJ: Wiley, 2001).
6   Edward T. Hall, *The Silent Language* (New York: Doubleday, 1959) and *The Hidden Dimension* (New York: Doubleday 1966).
7   A list of spaces needs a net-to-gross multiplier to estimate building size. This multiplier adds the space necessary for structure and walls (8–10 percent), circulation, and utilities. On complex, larger buildings this multiplier can nearly double the size of the building. On very small buildings, it can add as little as 15 to 20 percent.
8   Perkins and Will, Architects, Perspectives Charter School, Chicago, IL, 2004, in *Architectural Record* (2005).
9   California Department of Education. Retrieved August 25, 2016 at: www.cde.ca.gov/ls/fa/sf/completesch.asp.
10 The United States General Service Administration (GSA), Office of Government Policy, Office of Real Property Management, Performance Management Division, "Workspace Utilization and Allocation Benchmark." Benchmarking information for

different public and private office applications. Retrieved August 25, 2016 at: www.gsa.gov/graphics/ogp/Workspace_Utilization_Banchmark_July_2012.pdf.

11 Additional project costs include, but are not limited to: land acquisition, site utilities, utility hookup fees, debt servicing during construction, fees for zoning and building permits, testing during construction, project management time for owners and consultants, fees for architects and engineers, land surveys, environmental impact studies and mitigation costs, insurance, program changes, inflation, temporary accommodations during construction, furniture and equipment, move-in and activation costs, telecommunications, data systems, insurances and bonds, legal fees, contingencies. These "soft costs" or "ghost costs" commonly add 20 to 60 percent to the construction costs. Don't forget to add the cost of client time that would normally cover other duties.

12 The Department of Veterans Affairs Technical Information Library is a good source of information on health facilities. Retrieved August 25, 2016 at: www.cfm.va.gov/til/index.asp.

13 John R. Black, *The Toyota Way to Healthcare Excellence: Increase Efficiency and Improve Quality with Lean* (Chicago, IL: Health Care Administration Press, 2008).

14 Victoria Sweet, MD, *God's Hotel* (New York: Riverhead, 2012). Laguna Honda Hospital in San Francisco was one of the last Nightingale wards in use in the United States. This public hospital was used for long-term care of seriously ill patients.

15 Sources differ on the exact numbers, but all agree that nursing staff are doing more walking in single bedroom nursing units.

16 Retrieved August 25, 2016 at: www.pih.org/pages/butaro-hospital.

17 Mike Sheridan, "The Bay Area's Experimentation with Solving for Housing Affordability," *Urban Land: Magazine of the Urban Land Institute*, October 19, 2015. Retrieved August 25, 2016 at: http://urbanland.uli.org/planning-design/bay-areas-experimentation-solving-housing-affordability.

18 Gillem, Mark L. and Stacey Croll, "Housing with Dignity: A Post Occupancy Evaluation of Studios and Single Resident Occupancy Units in San Francisco" (School of Architecture and Allied Arts and the Tenderloin Neighborhood Development Corporation, December 2005).

Chapter 5
What Logic Orders
this Place?

*Architecture is organization. You are an organizer, not a
drawing-board artist.[1]*

Le Corbusier

Placemaking is about ordering the environment. Individuals
understand built form in a wide variety of ways. At the same
time most people recognize common elements, like paths,
edges, districts, nodes, and landmarks. Logics for making
places legible and meaningful depend on critical attention to
organizing movement, zones, and character.

Whose Logic?

Often when people think about what they need in a place,
they come up with a list of features, a laundry list of what
they want—a big kitchen, lots of storage, three bedrooms.
The designer thinks through these things and orders them
in a logical framework of relationships.

As a design team meets with an owner or a project
committee, the conversation may include a varied group of
stakeholders. Each of these individuals may bring a different
logic to the big table to identify the key elements and

Figure 5.1 *(facing page)*
Children Reading Map, Bill Hocker, photographer

assemble them into a new place. Some will be list-oriented and view this ordering much as a shopper would segregate fruits and vegetables from meats on a grocery list. Some will have specific priorities in mind, like replicating a place they know and enjoy. Engineers may want to organize the building into air-conditioned zones and naturally ventilated zones. Designers may have poetic metaphors, favorite geometric concepts, or principles of composition such as symmetry, rhythm, and contrast. Part of design is the stimulating activity of listening to all these ideas and integrating them.

Designing is a form of action anthropology. Designers immerse themselves in the culture of the people for whom they design. They try to create places that make sense and will be useful to the ultimate occupants. For example, during the design of a new blind rehabilitation center, a vision-impaired teacher requested that the new center take the shape of a capital letter. Their old building was in the shape of a capital F. This concept, admittedly not how the designer had experienced the building, led her to ponder the ways different people conceptualize space.[2] Learning from how the blind navigate a building added a layer of meaning for the sighted as well, demonstrating one of the logics that can be used to bring order to a place.

Individuals understand place and space very differently. The brain filters, organizes, and remembers what the senses collect and develops logical understandings. Taking a much broader approach than the traditional IQ test, Professor Howard Gardner's research group at the Harvard Graduate School of Education has identified multiple kinds of intelligence: verbal/linguistic, mathematical/logical, musical/rhythmic and harmonic, visual/spatial, bodily kinetic, interpersonal, intrapersonal, naturalistic, and existential. Most people have all these abilities in some sort of balance, but individuals can excel in one and not in another; for example, an athlete who flunks math or a poet who can't catch a ball. Although Gardner's work has been controversial, few doubt that cognitive differences affect people's logic and abilities.[3]

Individuals also experience the world differently depending their situation at the time: walking or driving a car, tired or energized, young or old. As people age, their experiences deepen—their abilities and perception of the world change as well. People filter their responses to the environment through their memories and make assumptions. People with impaired cognitive abilities, such as dementia, may lose their way figuratively and actually. They may perceive a door, but not remember where it leads.[4] What logics will make the environment more understandable and meaningful for all?

Common Logics

Despite this variation, people are more similar than different, and they share common logics. Designers seek these common understandings in order to design legible environments. Architect Kevin Lynch's seminal research, *The Image of the City*, offers one model of how people commonly understand space. Lynch set up an experiment to compare different people's images of downtown Boston, Jersey City, and Los Angeles. His team asked participants in each city to draw a map of their own downtown from memory. Researchers noted the order in which participants mapped city features and then followed up with interviews. The drawn maps were different from each other and also from the accurate map. When the maps were compared, the researchers found similarities as well as differences. They hypothesized that the elements of the city drawn by multiple people were elements that made the city legible to all. They analyzed the kinds of elements that recurred and categorized them: paths, edges, nodes, districts, and landmarks. Lynch's work remains highly

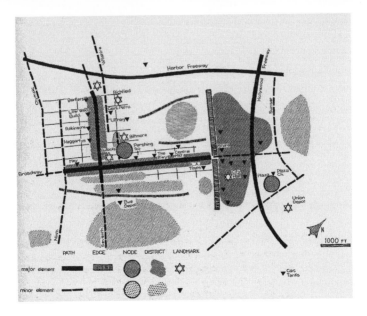

Figure 5.2
The visual form of Los Angeles as seen in the field, *The Image of the City*, Kevin Lynch

influential as a clear and logical vocabulary to describe environmental structure. It links how people understand places with the physical elements that compose cities, landscapes, neighborhoods, and buildings.

Movement, zoning, and character are three primary logics for organizing a place. Most places use all three elements. How the designer interprets a logic depends on the context of the project. Movement becomes more important as places have more parts. The design of flow is critical in urban design and building circulation, such as in a factory, where the layout of machines is primary. Zoning is a term for the legal mechanism used in clinical land use, but can also be used for the process of organizing a place. Separating clean areas from dirty areas may be essential in a laboratory building. Assigning space based on collaboration goals and hierarchy may be critical in an office building. Public and private is important in designing housing, but it will be very different in an American than in an Egyptian or Japanese home. Restaurant design depends on efficient flow and zoning in kitchens, but determining the character of the ambience is also an essential design logic.

Movement

Understanding flows of people, products, and vehicles is necessary to create logical understandable places. Lynch's studies identified paths as primary to the legibility of cities. London and Boston grew as interconnecting networks of major and minor paths with nodes and landmarks at points of decision. Paris and Washington, DC were master-planned with hub and spoke patterns. Many American cities developed as grids. An English student felt completely lost in the United States. He was used to navigating his small Cornish town by the hierarchy of curvilinear paths, where all streets led to the center. In an American grid plan, all the blocks seemed the same; lacking reference points, he could not find his way.

The egalitarian American grid can be relentless, the same for miles without spatial distinction among paths. Only the labels of the streets, sometimes by number in one direction and alphabet in the other, give cues. Where the grid is not the same in both directions, orientation is clearer. The magnificent New York City grid has long residential blocks running east–west and short commercial blocks running north–south, creating a pattern for easy navigation. In addition, the economic vitality of the heavily trafficked commercial avenues is supported by the residential cross-streets that feed into them.

Finding one's way in cities, neighborhoods, open spaces, and buildings has become so complex that a whole new

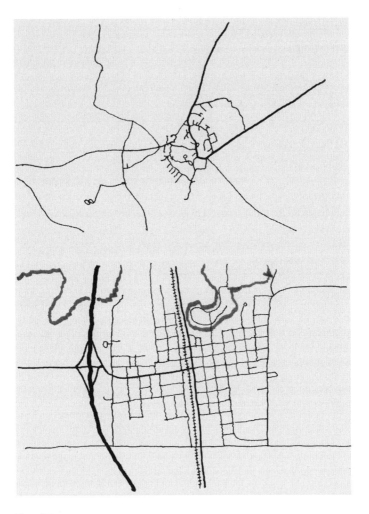

Figure 5.3
Two towns at the same scale each with about 1,550 residents: Stonesfield, Oxfordshire, United Kingdom, and Hillsboro, North Dakota, United States

profession in wayfinding has developed. Well-designed circulation gives people autonomy and agency. Although it is sometimes an adventure to get lost, confusion and frustration are seldom a design goal.[5] In recent years, the use of global positioning systems (GPS) has added a new layer of logic to finding one's way. Even complex paths can be followed step by step as long as the battery holds up. Are people losing autonomy and capability to navigate? Interestingly, the blind have gained agency from these GPS applications; their smartphones now read aloud both the wayfinding instructions step by step and the local signage.

Cues are essential to orientation as one moves around a city. It helps to see ahead to destinations and differentiate parts of a place by form and materials. For the blind, following curbs and path edges with a white cane keeps them on course. This system, known as shorelining, may break down where there is a discontinuity in the edge, an obstacle like a bench or a gap like an alcove. For the blind, making a wiggle in the edge or a change in surface texture may assist in navigation, just as for the sighted, visual landmarks at decision points show the way. People understand places by what stands out. An Italian colleague used the metaphor that a good city was like a cake with raisins.[6] The raisins are the landmarks: the elements with distinct forms, materials, and detailing that differentiate them from the fabric. The prominent domes of the churches of Rome, the Eiffel Tower, the Chrysler Building, Beijing's CCTV Headquarters, and Dubai's Burj Al Arab stand out as cultural landmarks, representing shifts in power among religious, industrial, commercial, and tourist interests. A similar logic within buildings organizes important rooms as landmarks in a fabric of minor rooms. For example, reading rooms in McKim, Mead & White's New York Public Library and Rem Koolhaas's Seattle Public Library are major places around which other spaces are located. At the scale of an indoor or outdoor room, distinct elements, such as the fireplace of Frank Lloyd

Wright's Robie House and the waterfall in New York's Paley Park, add focus and hierarchy.

In Lynch's terms, people recognize the "cake" as districts, places with form, color, and texture in common, and this also aids orientation. In a city or neighborhood, each district might have a repeating pattern of buildings with similar kinds of uses, of similar size, materials, and detailing. In buildings too, people know where they are, if parts are clear as districts. In an old building with multiple additions over the years, each wing may have a character that makes it distinct. For example, segments in a large hospital complex may be known as the 1960s wing, the new wing, the Bulfinch Building. Even though the result is one mega building, the parts are characteristically different. A clear path linking these districts makes a legible circulation system and an interesting journey. Inconsistencies often serve as landmarks benefiting navigation. People thrive in environments where journeys are rich, multisensory experiences.[7] Boring and anonymous cities and buildings make wayfinding difficult. Complexity and legibility are different attributes and are not mutually exclusive.

Zones

The logic of organizing space frequently identifies zones, which create useful adjacencies that serve social, economic, or functional goals. Some spaces need to be adjacent to others, like locker rooms next to swimming pools. In other circumstances, spaces may need to be separated or apart from other, like the music practice rooms in the basement at the Berklee School of Music, which are distant from the dormitory bedrooms. Temporal zones are convenient if portions of the building are open after hours such as an auditorium or a meeting room in a public library. Technical zones, like wet and dry, may simplify construction and save

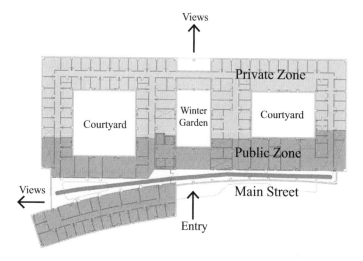

Figure 5.4
Zoning Diagram of a Medical Facility

money. Zones can be based on functional, temporal, technical, social, historical, and other differentiating features.

Often, discussion about adjacencies leads to questions about the larger social goals of a project. Should faculty offices in an architecture school be located near the studios, or should they be clustered in a separate wing? One scenario might encourage more faculty–student interaction, while the other more faculty–faculty exchange. Office layouts may be zoned by project, by job description, by work pattern, by seniority, and, of course, by rank in a hierarchy. In corporate institutions, the most important people may be higher in the building, often with special amenities like executive bathrooms and views. Reconsidering the hierarchy of the social structure as the primary logic for organizing a building would bring up other issues. It might be that productivity and employee retention would increase if people who are at their desks the most were located near the windows.

Similar activities in older cities tended to cluster together in functional groups. Rome is full of streets still called by the trade of those who lived and worked there. Modern cities, alas, still have zones where involuntary segregation persists, based on ethnic or racial background. Contemporary cities are formally zoned by use category, such as residential, commercial, or industrial. These regulations grew out of a desire to separate incompatible uses in the early twentieth century, when public health concerns emerged to challenge the mix of noisy, toxic, smelly, and hazardous industry with other activities.

In the post-World War II city, Jane Jacobs and others challenged this separation. In *The Death and Life of Great American Cities*, Jacobs argues for the vitality of cities with mixed uses. What cities need, she writes, "is the most intricate and close-grained diversity of uses that give each other constant mutual support, both economically and socially."[8] Many contemporary industries are less hazardous than those of the nineteenth century, and there is a growing interest in the return of manufacturing to the city. With manufacturing come jobs to support families, an important consideration in maintaining an inclusive city as downtowns gentrify.[9] In San Francisco, for example, where there is less industrially zoned land than previously, there are proposals to retain a certain percentage of land for industrial use. The century-old American logic of urban zoning is evolving as the nature of commerce, industry, and residential use change.

Temporal patterns of daily, weekly, and seasonal use can influence how a city, neighborhood, building, or room is designed. Jacobs argues that neighborhoods are livelier when they have at least two different kinds of primary businesses. The district, she writes, "must serve more than one primary function, preferably more than two. These must insure the presence of people who go outdoors on different schedules and are in the place for different purposes, but who are able to use many facilities in common."[10] Having two primary functions guarantees that small local businesses will have enough customers and that the street will be lively for a longer part of the day.

Architect and teacher Bill Kleinsasser used to teach that all places need backstages.[11] Most buildings have frontstage and backstage areas. The architect Louis Kahn, called these "served and servant" places.[12] People tend to think of buildings and places from the frontstage, or public side, which is experienced in memorable ways. People love the theater with its stage, but also love to take backstage tours of the workshops, dressing rooms, storerooms, and even green rooms where theater people gather. What is surprising is that backstage areas are often larger than frontstage areas. It is easy to underestimate the need for support spaces. Even people that live frugally and efficiently expect storerooms in the basement for bicycles, out-of-season goods, bulk purchases, and other items not in daily use. As novelist Maxine Hong Kingston said after a fire destroyed her home, if Americans want to appreciate a spare life with few belongings, they must do it quickly.[13] In this culture things accumulate fast—purchased, inherited, and given. The poorest accumulate too; they cannot afford to discard things they may need later.

Storage is one of the first needs mentioned by design clients. Backstage areas take many forms: cabinets, closets, tool sheds, attics, spare rooms, workshops, and even warehouses. Commercial rental storage units are now commonly available to provide remote backstage areas, which can range in size from an extra closet to a whole warehouse. The growth of this industry is a testament to the lack of backstage space in buildings and Americans' ability to accumulate belongings.

Character

The character of a place provides a multisensory, experiential logic. People understand places viscerally based on form scale, light, fragrance, sound, touch, and movement. Architecture Professor Stephen Duff likes to ask, "What is the feeling character" of this place?[14]

World travelers speak of the character of different neighborhoods and places in foreign cities. The different texture of life varies from arrondissement to arrondissement in Paris. People talk about the feel of each area, a feel that includes spatial as well as social characteristics—the width of the street, the height of the surrounding buildings—as well as textures, colors, culinary fragrances, trees, flowers in window boxes, the languages and music heard, the size of the dogs, the general upkeep and graffiti, and other factors.

At the University of California, Berkeley, at a time when many new buildings were being added, Campus Landscape Architect Ortha Zebroski organized the campus by a system of characteristic landscapes. She identified five patterns to implement: ornamental flower borders around lawns, riparian vegetation, xeroscape plantings with minimal watering needs, indigenous plants, and sports fields.[15] These choices guide landscape designers and staff to make outdoor places that support different experiences and uses, while operating within an understandably limited budget. Drought risk is always present in coastal California, so areas featuring native plants and xeroscape are favored. Areas with ornamental horticulture are few, but delightful when encountered.

Spatial character is often a crucial logic employed in establishing an organizational brand. When Oregon's Umpqua Bank rebranded itself to separate itself from its competition, they imagined a bank that was more like a retail store. In designing this new character, they focussed on everything from site selection to interior details and programed activities.

Figure 5.5
Traces, the Therme, Vals, Peter Zumthor, architect, Alison Kwok, photographer

Umpqua selects storefronts with lots of windows. Once inside, concierge desks, not tellers' windows, greet customers. Designed to be places to be and to linger, the branches feature coffee bars and host community activities. The urban legend, backed by the bank's statistics, is that the redesign has contributed to the bank's skyrocketing assets and high employee retention rate.[16]

Architect Peter Zumthor's thermal baths at Vals, Switzerland, demonstrate how experientially rich a place can be when character drives its logic. The journey spirals around a warm central pool with nine blue skylights and ends in an outdoor pool with framed views to the mountains beyond. Bathers pass doorways to different rooms with various pools along the way, like the tall, narrow red-walled room full of the hottest water, with noise from the machinery that heats it—a veritable devil's lair; the blue room with the cold plunge, entered by gentle steps against which water laps; a grotto of rough-textured rock one bends under a low lintel to reach. Sinuous rosewood benches for lounging, black rubber curtains and stools, bronze handrails and waterspouts further intensify the range of sensual experiences. The architect wanted to incorporate taste; one room is a place to drink the waters from hanging bronze mugs.

The benefits of character add to the logics of organization of movement and zones. Good places need all three. Design is an iterative process that superimposes ideas to create a place. A place without an underlying and clear logic may be amusing, but can be confusing, and ultimately, may not be useful or valued. People love *Alice in Wonderland*, but may not want to live there. At the same time, a place that can be totally understood at a glance will not add much richness to people's lives, compared to one that embodies layers of thinking that may only be revealed over time.

Notes

1 Le Corbusier, "If I Had to Teach You Architecture," *Focus*, 1938, as quoted in Christopher Alexander and Serge Chermayeff, *Community and Privacy* (New York: Anchor, Doubleday, 1965), 103.

2 Blind architect Christopher Downey and author Christie Johnson Coffin, conversations during the design of the Veterans Administration Western Blind Rehabilitation Center.

3 Howard Gardner, *Frames of Mind, The Theories of Multiple Intelligences*, 3rd ed. (New York: Basic Books, 2011), with a new introduction by the author. First published in 1983.

4 John Zeisel, *I'm Still Here: A New Philosophy of Alzheimer's Care* (New York: Avery, 2009).

5 Gerald Weisman, "Designing to Orient the User," *Architecture, the AIA Journal*, 78, no. 10 (1989): 109–110.

6 Rosaria Hodgdon, Associate Professor of Architecture, University of Oregon.

7 "The Journey," lecture by Edward Allen, University of Oregon, January 16, 2004.

8 Jane Jacobs, *The Death and Life of Great American Cities* (New York: Vintage Books, Random House, 1961), 14.

9 Professor Howard Davis, conversations about inclusive urbanism with author Jenny Young.

10 Jane Jacobs, *The Death and Life of Great American Cities*, 152.

11 Professor William Kleinsasser, conversations with the authors.

12 Architect Louis Kahn's coworkers and students credit Kahn with this terminology.

13 Maxine Hong Kingston, lecture, the Portland Arts and Letters Series, Portland, Oregon, January 9, 1992. Retrieved August 25, 2016 at: www.literary-arts.org/archive/maxine-hong-kingston.

14 Stephen Duff, Associate Professor of Architecture, University of Oregon.

15 Ortha Zebroski, Campus Landscape Architect, University of California, Berkeley, 1989–1996. In conversations with author Christie J. Coffin.

16 Robert Walker, "Branching Out," *New York Times*, September 24, 2006; Paul Sweeney, "Business Diary: I'll Take a Double Latte and a Personal Loan," *New York Times*, September 26, 1999. First store design: Stern Marketing Group of Berkeley, California, Charlotte Stern, president (1999); subsequent stores' design: ZIBA, Portland, Oregon (2005–).

Figure 6.1
Bryant Park, New York City, Noelle E. Jones, photographer

Chapter 6
Does this Place Balance Community and Privacy?

No [hu]man is an island, entire of itself. Every [hu]man is a piece of the continent, a part of the main.[1]

John Donne

I want to be alone.[2]

Greta Garbo

Open/enclosed, small/large, simple/complicated, wasteful/frugal, loud/quiet, adult friendly/family friendly, stimulating/peaceful, decorated/plain: A place can be described along a spectrum of any one of these dichotomies and many others as well. Of the various possible gradients, public/private is one of the most important. How places support and balance needs for both community and privacy are questions for every designer in every project.

Psychiatrist Humphry Osmond talks about places that foster community and bring people together, which he calls sociopetal; and places that separate or isolate people and discourage community, which he calls sociofugal. A wavy bench can be sociopetal where it is concave, allowing people to face each other, and sociofugal where it is convex, positioning people to face outward. Osmond argues that traditional markets, like farmers' markets and community markets, are sociopetal, but that supermarkets are sociofugal. He measured this phenomenon, counting more interactions of people in a community market and fewer in a supermarket.[3]

Figure 6.2
Sociopetal and Sociofugal Bench, Jenny Young, photographer

Community

People exist in cultural contexts rooted in community. These
social communities are nested or overlapped, some by kinship
but many by affinity and lifestyle. Community is not a luxury
but an essential ingredient for survival. People need each
other for support, companionship, intimacy, and health.
Individuals isolated, such as those in solitary confinement,
risk losing their basic humanity.[4]

Often the first thing people build in new communities
is a school or place of worship for gathering. In the early
part of the twentieth century, when women were entering
universities, working, and gaining the vote, many formed
clubs and built clubhouses. New immigrants in a city often

create meeting halls for people like themselves, who speak their language literally and/or figuratively. Situating a community physically in space can add meaning and longevity to that community.

Communities change and community places are often repurposed. In Berkeley, California, a building that had housed an active Jewish congregation is now a Dominican seminary. A formerly active Protestant church with a major Sunday school building has been transformed into a liberal arts Islamic college. Across the country, Elks Lodges, historically men's clubs, now have video sports bars and provide RV parking, where travelers can plug in as they caravan from state to state. Agricultural environmentalists have adopted the San Luis Obispo Grange as their community center, in part because the Grange building existed. A roll call in any community will reveal some unusual affinity groups. Homeschooling parents in Eugene, Oregon, as one example, have built a school, in part, because they felt their children were not developing useful social skills. Even in this digital age, most individuals see a need for a physical place to reflect and solidify their existence, customs, and membership and meet with sympathetic others.

Knowing which activities bring people together and locating them strategically is the seed for making places for community. The kitchen table in a house becomes a magnet for social life. The village well of historic towns became the gathering place for people to talk; public squares developed in conjunction with where wells were located. What is the best place to locate an office coffee/tea center to encourage informal communication?

Coffee shops, bars, exercise rooms, libraries, schools, places of worship, and restaurants are all places where specific activities bring people together. A successful after-hours place in Taipei, Taiwan, is the Eslite Book Store, open 24/7 with coffee and light foods. Friends meet there.

Figure 6.3
Gràcia Neighborhood Square, Barcelona, Jenny Young, photographer

The auditorium is available for events and concerts. The bookstore functions as a successful, air-conditioned, public place, positioned near major paths with multiple connections to the city around it. It supports a range of human activity—very private reading in a corner between bookcases, more active browsing of current periodicals on open racks, and sitting and enjoying a coffee with friends at café tables.

Successful Italian piazzas, Mexican zocalos, or university quadrangles depend on a variety of uses to draw people there. Like the Eslite Book Store, they succeed because they are positioned near major paths with multiple connections to the urban fabric surrounding them. Public squares are places for many kinds of community events, demonstrations, concerts, and markets, but a successful square has places for individuals and small groups, too. People feel comfortable because, although they are outdoors, they feel contained. The edges give people places to establish themselves without being on full display. Individuals can position themselves, observe the world going by or immerse themselves in their own thoughts, a newspaper, a cellphone. Arcades and umbrellas covering small groups of tables and chairs create smaller places with rain and sun protection. These are the places people go to first. Once people are there, they prime the space for others to come and feel comfortable.[5]

Locating places in positions where multiple paths cross increases their chance to become social centers.[6] Urban design professor Bill Hillier leads the Space Syntax Laboratory that maps street networks. The number of paths and the connections that make a place accessible to other places in the network identifies locations most likely to support community. To figure out the best place to locate the new millennial footbridge across the Thames, the group analyzed the path network in London, modeling congestion and movement patterns. They then advised the city to position architect Norman Foster's new bridge to link

Figure 6.4
Millennium Bridge, London, Norman Foster, architect, Howard Davis, photographer

---

Figure 6.5
Piazza della Rotonda, Rome, Bill Hocker, photographer

St. Paul's Cathedral to the Tate Modern Gallery. Their analysis predicted that the chosen location would result in 4.4 million people crossing the bridge per year, but by 2006 over 9 million were crossing annually.[7]

Too much vehicular street traffic can affect the quality of community and privacy. Landscape architect Donald Appleyard studied three residential streets closely and analyzed interactions quantitatively and qualitatively. Where there is very little traffic, a neighborhood street can be a social center and support community interactions. Where there is a lot of traffic, people do not tend to know their neighbors across the street, though they may know neighbors to either side or across backyard fences.[8]

As discussed in Chapter 4, size matters. Boston City Hall Plaza is an example of a public space that is too big, even for a large city like Boston. From the time it opened in 1968, people have been making proposals to improve it. In 2005, the Project for Public Spaces ranked it as one of the "Squares Most in Need of Improvement in the United States." Size is not the only problem of Boston City Hall Plaza. How space is outfitted and detailed is important too. Places that foster community are rich with details that make people comfortable and add interest and meaning. Chairs at cafés, benches, and steps are anchors for people to root themselves. Fountains or sculptures become props that people can lean on, open to the spectacle and drama of human life. Decorative motifs, symbols, and historic memorials contribute to community identity.[9]

Privacy

Privacy is as basic a consideration as community. People desire, need, and, now in many places, have the right to be able to decide what information about themselves should be shared with others. Privacy allows people to set themselves apart from others as they strive for identity. It is hard to imagine a world without private places for concentration, reflection, meditation, sleep, and just relaxation from the demands of social life. Virginia Woolf argues "a room of one's own"[10] is necessary to enable a woman to write and become her own person.

Degrees of privacy have changed over time and are different in different contexts. People today are both startled and intrigued by the lack of privacy in one-room pioneer cabins, houses in developing countries, or even middle-class apartments in New York City or Taiwan. Where space itself is a luxury, people may not expect much physical privacy in their lives but may devise social mechanisms to achieve privacy. In Taiwan, sweethearts have become aficionados of karaoke parlors, where they can rent by the hour a small room and select music to sing with. It is said that these parlors have contributed to population growth in Taiwan. There are some contexts, where the amount of privacy needs to be controlled. In mental health facilities, places with privacy can bring risks of violence and suicide for the seriously ill. In public parks and daycare centers, requirements for supervision balance with needs for privacy.

Places that support privacy are usually differentiated spatially. Positioning elements off the main path or at the end of the path can make them more private. A twisting indirect entry path increases privacy, as in an Islamic house. Adding layers that filter—walls, partial walls, and screens—can augment privacy by shielding people from surrounding activities.

Complete enclosure offers visual, acoustic, and olfactory privacy. Enclosure is what a teenager and her family might want for her room, or what a European expects in a toilet stall. Different kinds of privacy[11] may require different design responses; for example, soundproof glass may provide needed acoustic privacy but retain visual connections. Places that are smaller, lower, softly lighted, and quiet can feel more private.

In open office layouts that are too quiet, people may be afraid to talk as any sound would be overheard and be disruptive. A common technique is to introduce white noise to make the environment feel more private, so that people believe their conversations will not be heard.

Community and Privacy

Spatial variety and ambience can reinforce a gradient of public-to-private space. People want opportunities for both: places that support community and places for privacy. In many buildings, the logical organization of space follows an "intimacy gradient."[12] This logic is particularly true in a house that is organized from a public entrance that leads into the most public parts of the house, where strangers are welcomed for socializing, to the most private parts of the house, typically the bedrooms and bathrooms.

Edges can become places that balance community and privacy. When working on projects, people often choose to meet at a kitchen or dining room table, so they can be at the heart of the action. When it is time to sit down to eat, things have to be cleared and put to one side. *A Pattern Language* describes that conflict:

> The opposing needs for some community and some seclusion at the same time in the same space, occur in almost every family. ... People want to be together, but at the same time they want the opportunity for some small amount of privacy, without giving up community. ... To give a group a chance to be together, as a group, a room must also give them the chance to be alone, in one's and two's in the same space.[13]

The alcoves advocated in *A Pattern Language* help balance space for community with space for privacy.

Architect Louis Kahn's library on the campus of Phillips Exeter Academy in Exeter, New Hampshire, is famous as a building whose spatial structure and material development make tangible its purpose, a library for students. In Kahn's words, "A [hu]man with a book goes to the light. A library begins that way."[14] Books are a community resource that all can access, but using books is a private activity of focus and reflection. The spatial structure of the Exeter Library differentiates a public and communal center from private zones for reading. The central public area is a square atrium, a tall volume with diffuse reflected light. Precious travertine paves the floor and inscribes the walls with enormous circles beyond which are several floors of book stacks. The ring of book stacks is a series of low floors made of reinforced concrete, functional for carrying the weight of the books. Beyond the stacks and at the edge of the building is a zone of private study carrels, well lit by tall clerestory windows. Pairs of private carrels, elegantly detailed in wood and each with its own view window, are inset against exterior walls of loadbearing brick, the material of most other campus buildings. As Kahn once said, "In a small room one does not say what one would in a large room,"[15]—the design of the spaces reinforces that difference from communal center to private edge.

Rosa Parks Elementary School[16] in Berkeley, California, was planned as a community school. Each classroom is a community for twenty to thirty children with one teacher and sometimes a parent volunteer, teacher's aide, or visitor. It is theirs to use and control, to decorate as they develop traditions for the school year. The classroom is a house-shaped "home." The scale is comfortable both when few are there and when crammed with parents on back-to-school night. The place can support a small community of students and also provide privacy from the larger school.

Each classroom has its own patio. These small places shelter not just individuals or small groups but provide a

Figure 6.6
Schoolyard, Rosa Parks School, Berkeley, California, Ratcliff (Christie Johnson Coffin and Kava Massih), architects, Jenny Young, photographer

Figure 6.7   Model of Rosa Parks School, Ratcliff, architects

Does this Place Balance Community and Privacy?

place for botanical experiments, small pets like frogs, activities too messy for indoors, and really anything the teacher wants to include and maintain. Each classroom also has a small secondary space it shares with the next classroom, a teacher's office or workroom, where volunteers, specialists, and others can meet with students individually or in very small groups. It can be a "time out" place for a disruptive child. It can be a small group space for project work.

At a larger scale, five to seven classrooms are clustered around a courtyard with picnic benches and access to toilets for children. There are three grade school clusters and a cluster for kindergarten and preschool children. At this scale, a school within a school can happen, such as a Spanish–English bilingual school that truly immerses children in both languages. Respect for both languages and cultures is not just taught but experienced. When bilingual kids have their own place in the larger school, both languages are heard at recess. The school as a whole works not as a melting pot but as a mosaic. Different communities can be formed with different intentions to support both children and teachers.

The school's three playgrounds bring larger communities of children and teachers together. A large grassy sports field is shared with the city and is also a public park after hours. Grade school children use the central, circular playground. The kindergarten and preschool have their own playground and vegetable garden, where small children will not be run down by fifth graders. Again, there is a sense of community and also a relationship to the next scale of community. The principal's office has a view of the grade school playground and is near the front door, where he stands ready to welcome and help. To the side of the main entrance is the multi-purpose room with its arguably impossible confluence of roles: gymnasium, cafeteria, music room, auditorium, public meeting room, and, inevitably, a locus for afterschool programs. This room opens to the public park with enormous doors to reach out to the neighborhood. On the other street edges, the classrooms, like little houses, sit comfortably in the surrounding residential community.

Not surprisingly, this well-developed public-to-private gradient grew out of a series of community workshop sessions that included neighbors, parents, children, teachers, and a large and diverse design team. The design team provided childcare, Spanish translation, and food. People said things like: Don't put anything noisy in that corner, because the man who lives there is so nice to the school. As a result, the quiet sides of several classrooms face his house. The commitment to listening to community ended up being reflected in a school designed and built to support community. Rosa Parks Elementary School is a place about community and for community, but there are opportunities for privacy throughout. Uncovering the appropriate balance between community and privacy is a critical part of any design.

Notes

1 John Donne, "Meditation 13," *Devotions upon Emergent Occasions* (1624). Retrieved August 25, 2016 at: https://en.wikiquote.org/wiki/John_Donne.

2 Greta Garbo, *Grand Hotel* (1932). Retrieved August 25, 2016 at: www.youtube.com/watch?v=tojjWQvlPN8.

3 Humphry Osmond's work is discussed by Robert Sommer, "Theoretical Influences," in *Social Design: Creating Buildings with People in Mind* (Upper Saddle River, NJ: Prentice Hall, 1983), 42–45.

4 Atul Gawande, "Hellhole," *New Yorker*, March 30, 2009. Retrieved August 25, 2016 at: www.newyorker.com/magazine/2009/03/30/hellhole.

5 Donald Corner and Jenny Young, "The Italian Piazza: A Model for Comprehensive Analysis," paper presented at the International Seminar on Urban Form, Rome, Italy, September 2015.

6 Kevin Lynch named these places "nodes."

7 Randy Gragg, "London's Large-Scale Regeneration Projects Offer Community Benefits," *Land Lines*, 18, no. 4 (October 2005).

8 Donald Appleyard and Mark Lintell, "The Environmental Quality of City Streets: The Residents' View Point," Environmental Design Research Association (EDRA

2003), fig. 4, 11-2-7. Retrieved August 25, 2016 at: www.edra.org/sites/default/files/publications/EDRA03-Appleyard-11-2_0.pdf.

9   Corner and Young, "The Italian Piazza."

10   Virginia Woolf, *A Room of One's Own* (New York: Harcourt Brace Jovanovich, 1981). First published in 1929.

11   Jon T. Lang, "Privacy, Territoriality, and Personal Space: Proxemic Theory," in *Creating Architectural Theory: The Role of the Behavioral Sciences in Environmental Design* (New York: Van Nostrand Reinhold, 1987), 145–146. Alan Westin categorizes privacy in four types: solitude, intimacy, anonymity and reserve.

12   Christopher Alexander, Sara Ishikawa, Murray Silverstein et al., "Intimacy Gradient," in *A Pattern Language* (New York, Oxford University Press, 1977), 610–613.

13   Christopher Alexander et al., "Alcoves," *A Pattern Language*, 828–832.

14   Louis I. Kahn and Alessandra Latour, *Louis I. Kahn: Writings, Lectures, Interviews* (New York: Rizzoli, 1981).

15   Louis Kahn, in conversation with architects, who worked in Kahn's architectural office.

16   Ratcliff, Project Architects Christie J. Coffin and Kava Massih, Rosa Parks Elementary School (formerly called Columbus Elementary School), Berkeley, California, 1998. Several articles have described this school: Karen Franck and Teresa von Sommaruga Howard, *Design through Dialogue: A Guide for Architects and Clients* (New York: Wiley, 2010); Henry Sanoff, "Accessibility in a Community School," evaluation of Rosa Parks School, in *Schools Designed with Community Participation* (Washington, DC: National Clearinghouse for Education Facilities, 2002), 49–57; Todd Bressi, "Rosa Parks Elementary School," *Places*, 14, no. 1 (Winter 2001): 6–9.

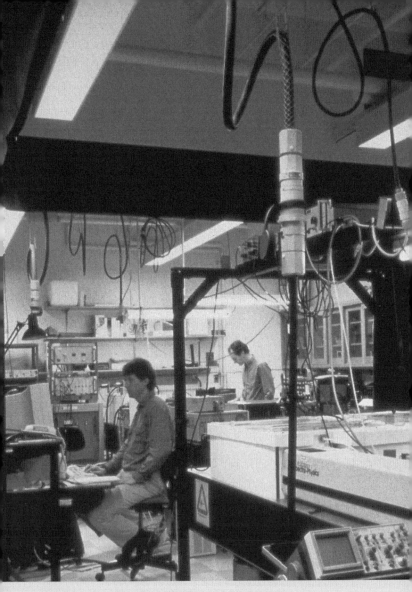

Figure 7.1
Physics Laboratory, Christie Johnson Coffin, photographer

Chapter 7
What Makes this
Place Useful?

*Ah, the bossy building. My contention is that architecture
cannot make you do anything, but it sure can prevent you
from doing things. An example: A bench in a hallway can't
make you stop and talk to your neighbors, but no bench
in the hallway sure discourages it. Same for housing near
transit—can't make you take the train, but if you don't live
near it, you won't take it.[1]*

Judith Wasserman

What makes a place a useful tool? All places channel
behaviors and exclude behaviors by how they are made. A
place can contribute to productivity and creativity, or it can
get in the way and limit efforts. What makes a place bossy?
Bossy places control behavior, erect barriers, and limit the
ability of people to do their best. A well-designed place can
provide a nudge that guides users to good results and offer
cues to support better performance.

Efficiency and Flow

Think of the American kitchen, as structured by pioneering
industrial engineer and efficiency expert Lillian Gilbreth.[2]
Gilbreth's analysis of household cooking led to using a
triangle formed by refrigerator, sink, and stove as the basis
for middle-class, American kitchens. Working in a kitchen

without this basic triangle is frustrating for a cook used to this convenience. Does it channel behavior? Certainly. As with many commonly practiced forms, it carries history. It was formulated largely for a single cook in the kitchen, at a time when the middle class was growing and no longer employed maids. Does it support multiple cooks in the kitchen? Not always. Although the basic working triangle remains the backbone of appliance layout, contemporary kitchens often feature islands and peninsulas, where cooks can talk to each other as they prepare a meal together.

Designing a suite of rooms for surgery is another case where functional requirements determine the layout of the place. Surgery departments are carefully zoned to support differing levels of sterile technique, different casts of characters, different clothing, and different management streams for clean, sterile, and soiled activities and materials. New digital tools contribute by tracking people and objects in an effort to eliminate the risk of mistakes and wasted motion.

Put simply, an inpatient surgical suite is built on evidence that almost everything has to be close to almost everything else. Surgical operations thrive on the availability of materials, instruments, and expert practitioners in close proximity. The result is a tightly organized puzzle-like layout that makes any kind of change very tricky and expensive. Every discipline has clear turf. Every piece of equipment has a place. Flow of materials and people with different roles is optimized. A fully engineered American surgery department is full of cues helpful for maintaining good sterile technique and good surgical practices.[3]

The ironic thing is that when a surgery department is observed in operation, the people using it apparently did not read the manual. They use it differently from the way it was conceived. Changes in staffing, equipment, surgical practice, quality control measures, waste removal, and materials management are ongoing and with them are some different

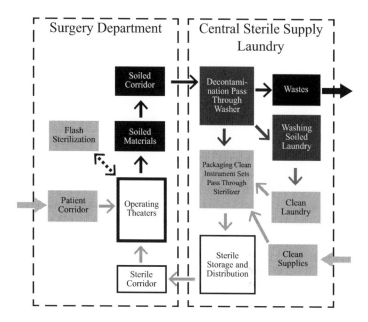

Figure 7.2
Flow diagram for the surgery and central sterile supply departments

environmental needs. "Why didn't the designers ask us?" the
staff wonders. The senior nurses, managers, and surgeons—
none of whom really had time for committee work—were
asked. Yet, in spite of this, the department is working;
patients are being treated and recovering. Designers may
have planned for a different year's needs, but the department
works. Intelligent staff have not allowed themselves to be
bossed around by the building and have figured out how to
make it all work remarkably well. In fact, army field
hospitals in tents also work well with many fewer nudges,
but most professionals would find maintaining good surgical
practices under those circumstances stressful.

Flow is also essential in eye care and other medical
treatment. The very efficient Aravind Eye Care System[4]

provides an unusual volume of high quality, compassionate care in Tamil Nadu, India. Motivated by the enormous problem of needless, untreated blindness in India, the founder, ophthalmologist G. Venkataswamy (known as Dr. V), attended McDonald's Hamburger University in Oak Brook, Illinois, and learned approaches for analyzing and organizing flows to support higher volume and maintain quality.

Clinics in Aravind eye hospitals are organized in a linear path with multiple testing stations to screen for problems, refract and provide eyeglasses, and identify candidates for surgery. If cataract surgery is indicated, patients can usually be treated the next morning. Each day a large volume of urban and rural patients receive surgery. More than half are treated essentially free, paying as little as bus fare. Those who can pay market rates. In the surgery department, preparation, surgery, and recovery are supervised by Aravind-trained ophthalmic nurses. The nurses make it possible for the surgeons to move smoothly from one patient to the next with no wasted time. Operating rooms in early years accommodated as many as six operating tables to improve productivity and to share expensive surgical microscopes. The microscope was mounted on a ceiling track allowing it to slide into place on the next table as soon as the previous surgery was complete. Dormitories are available for rural patients, who stay a few days after surgery for antibiotic drops to avoid the risk of eye infection on the dusty bus ride home. Many older adults have regained their sight and productive roles in their communities.

The Aravind system has treated more than 35 million patients and now performs 400,000 surgeries each year. Quality of care provided by Aravind is excellent with infection rates comparable to those in the United Kingdom. The Aravind business model has been studied extensively. They have developed a graduate program that teaches leaders throughout Asia and Africa to do as they do: diagram the process in detail, monitor productivity on a daily basis,

Figure 7.3
Waiting Room, Aravind Eye Hospital, Madurai, India, Christie Johnson Coffin, photographer

monitor quality, follow a policy of continuous improvement, and always practice with compassion.[5]

A new Aravind Eye Hospital in Chennai will follow this tradition and like other Aravind Hospitals has a large, central courtyard. In this case, a thirty-second walk on a bridge over the courtyard between operating rooms and recovery rooms is a positive break of daylight and greenery, introducing a celebration of sight into the efficient layout.[6]

Creativity and Productivity

Productivity is not only about efficiency and flow but also about creativity and innovation. Creativity and profitability are said to be encouraged today by the polished workplaces built for Amazon, Apple, Facebook, Google, Microsoft, and other high-end technology companies. The new industry standards for workplace design have been set by prestigious designers.[7] The new company campuses provide landscaped milieus replete with sportsfields, running tracks, excellent food, childcare, gardens, light and air, and competitive well-trained colleagues. Staff in some cases are offered a menu of different workplaces: yurts, cubes, cafés, huddles, caves, phone booths, tables, even desks. Workers need never go home, but telecommuting is also an option.

Facebook's new campus features a single, enormous room, where 2,800 people work with CEO Mark Zuckerberg's desk in the middle.[8] Apple's new spaceship is a 1.6-kilometer circumference (1-mile) doughnut. This infinite loop is almost half the size of the Pentagon and will house 13,000 employees. Amazon's new home includes what looks like a biosphere in downtown Seattle. Proximity of staff, security for intellectual property, efficiency, economy, and amenity are all goals in the design of these places.

Certainly these companies are enormously successful, in large part due to their ability to attract talented professionals. What is the contribution of these new workplaces? Who is going to measure the role these places play in the success? Internal knowledge is proprietary and not available. These locked campuses provide the press with carefully selected photographs and little opportunity for critical review. The new high-tech campuses encourage their employees to live at work, isolating them in a monoculture of young technical workers.

What is the contribution of these new larger open spaces to the workers and the companies? The special creative enclaves are often off-campus in anonymous locations. Many have found small groups, maybe four to eight people, sharing a space, a creative milieu. Creativity can flourish in the family garage, a loft, an empty storefront, or a warehouse. Hewlett-Packard began in a one-car garage, and a generation later Jobs and Wozniak started Apple in the Jobs'

Figure 7.4
Pacific Film Archive offices, Berkeley, California, Diller, Scofidio + Renfro Architects,
Stephen Coffin, photographer

family garage. When asked to describe what they wanted
their lab spaces to be like, the experimental physicists for the
University of Oregon Science Buildings asked for labs like
double garages, unencumbered spaces with access to lots of
electricity.

In some ways, the new high-tech campuses are less
like the founders' creative enclaves and more like
nineteenth-century company towns. Enlightened
industrialists built towns like Port Sunlight, Merseyside,
United Kingdom; Pullman, Illinois; and Gilchrist, Oregon.
They believed that their factory production of soap, railroad
cars, or lumber would improve if their workers were well
housed and well fed. George Pullman hoped an "ordered and
beautiful" environment would "uplift" its residents.[9] New
towns provided worker and manager housing, stores, and
public buildings for edification and recreation, such as
schools, post offices, an art gallery in Port Sunlight, a
bowling alley in Gilchrist. Accounts of life in these towns
also include stories of paternalism; a company town lacks
the politics of a more democratically administered
community.

Slack and Fit

The use of places is seldom fully predictable. As discussed in Chapter 2, planning for the future is helpful, if imprecise. Few companies and institutions stand still, and crystal balls are notoriously unreliable. If a commercial building can be configured to work for both tremendous success and growth and for serious enterprise contraction, it may keep open more options for the future. A place should fit the use, but some slack is really helpful given the rate of change with which people inevitably live.

Too tight a fit can create problems. Changes in codes and program needs benefit from a bit of slack. Some designers enjoy the challenge of providing code minimum and not one bolt, square meter, or feature more. This may save the client in first costs, but may also hasten the day when renovations are mandated to meet new needs, codes, and standards.

Sometimes a bit of slack or generosity in design can give a building adaptability. In his houses, architect William Wurster had a habit of including a room that did not have a name or a programmed need. Families have used this room-without-a-name in many different ways: art studio, guest room, family room, play room, music room, in-law or nanny accommodation.[10] Having this room made a modestly sized Wurster house friendly to the life of a family, as it changed over time. Wurster's graceful houses tend to be treasured and serve inhabitants for many years with little need for renovation. A more recent example is architect Michael Pyatok's practice of positioning a bedroom and bath near the front door in many of his affordable housing projects. This location makes that bedroom work equally well as an office, a rented room, or a grandparent's place.[11]

Control and Choice

Places both control behavior and provide choices. At one end of the spectrum, prisons are organized to prohibit socially unacceptable behavior, control violent criminals, and keep staff safe. The ultimate control is in the supermax prison, where prisoners are held in solitary confinement, often for years, with little or no social contact. The supermax maximizes control and minimizes choice. Atul Gawande recounts research that describes how years of solitary confinement destroy personality, making individuals unfit for society. Individuals, if not already incorrigible, might well be after supermax tenure. The building is indeed a punishment, which Gawande convincingly describes as cruel and unusual. Although 25,000 prisoners are currently held in supermax prisons in the United States, it is not clear that the use of supermax for the most violent has reduced the overall number and seriousness of violent incidents within prisons.[12] Unintentional effects limit their value. Ideas about prisons are changing, and these buildings with their concrete cells will not be easily adapted or humanized.

At the other end of the spectrum from the supermax prison are many underutilized and undervalued structures. Unused storefronts, workshops, light industrial buildings, and warehouses can in creative hands accommodate ad hoc adaptation without controversy or extreme cost. Want a hole in the wall? Go ahead. Need a new partition? A quick bit of do-it-yourself and a place is built. Innovative arts groups have done very well with these kinds of buildings. One example is the Temporary Contemporary in Los Angeles, an open warehouse that was used as an interim building during the construction of the permanent Museum of Contemporary Art (MOCA). After MOCA opened, people recognized there was still a need for the Temporary Contemporary's wide, tall spaces that could be reconfigured for every show. Exhibitions that cannot find a comfortable home in the elegant MOCA continue to value the freedom and flexibility of the Temporary Contemporary.[13]

Places can be planned anywhere on a spectrum from fixed and controlling to flexible and enabling. Victorian townhouses in London occupy a midpoint and have maintained their utility over time. They were designed as houses and flats in a rapidly urbanizing culture. Today they are able to accommodate a wide range of uses from actual residential use to shops, professional offices, and even a well-known architecture school, the Architectural Association. What makes them work so well? They provide rooms that accommodate small groups of people working or living together. A clear circulation system of central, open staircases connects these rooms without imposing a particular organization among them. Because many row houses adjoin, several buildings can be linked to make a larger fabric of accommodations. They have distinctive historic character that provides identity for resident groups. Of course, these places can be unpleasantly bossy, if they are a bad fit for an organization's particular needs.

Historic places that have been reused have lessons for designers today who want to ensure the places they design will have utility in the future. Consider one element that most historic buildings have: operable windows. With contemporary electric light and mechanical air-conditioning systems, building designers can eliminate the choice of daylight and natural ventilation for inhabitants. Wouldn't people rather decide that for themselves? Windows can be blacked out when required, as many an ophthalmologist has done. In University of Oregon laser labs, light-tight window shutters cut out light during experiments, which may last days or weeks, and open to provide light during setup, which may take weeks or months.

How can we make places functional tools to help people do what they need? How can we avoid erecting barriers to individual choice? How can we exclude undesired behavior and foster desired behavior? Good, enduring places are conversational, not bossy. They provide both slack and fit. They provide the friendly nudge and don't limit opportunity.

Notes

1 Private communication, August 1, 2013 with Judith Wasserman, architect with Bressack and Wasserman Architects, Los Altos, CA.
2 Many know Lillian Gilbreth not for her key role in the development of scientific management or her pioneering time and motion studies (often with her husband Frank Gilbreth and twelve children), but from a popular book written by two of her twelve children, Frank B. Gilbreth, Jr., and Ernestine Gilbreth Carey, *Cheaper by the Dozen* (New York: Thomas Y. Crowell, 1948; New York: Harper Perennial Modern Classics, repr. ed., 2002).
3 A good source on medical facility design is the United States Department of Veterans Affairs Technical Information Library (http://va.gov/til). Guidelines for many departments are available and are updated in rotation; not all information is up to date.
4 Available online at: www.aravind.org.
5 V. Kasturi Rangan, "Aravind Eye Hospital, Madurai, India: In Service to Sight," *Harvard Business School Case*, April 1, 1993, revised: May 15, 2009.
6 Christie Johnson Coffin, "Architectural Considerations for Designing, Constructing or Renovating Eye Care Facilities for High Quality, Large Volume, Sustainable Cataract Surgery", Architectural Module for the *Quality Cataracts Series* (Madurai, Tamil Nadu, India: Aravind/Seva Publications, 2001). Coffin has worked with Seva Foundation and Aravind Eye Care System since the mid-1990s, including the conceptual design for the Aravind Eye Hospital, Chennai, working with Design Collaborative, Pondicherry, India, Israel Gnanaraj, architect.
7 Apple has worked with Foster & Associates, Amazon and Microsoft with NBBJ, Google with BIG and Heatherwick Studio, Facebook with Frank Gehry.
8 Zach Wener-Fligner, *Quartz*. Retrieved August 26, 2016 at: http://qz.com/373448/photos-facebooks-new-headquarters-designed-by-frank-gehry/oogle.
9 Stanley Buder, "The Model Town of Pullman: Town Planning and Social Control in the Gilded Age," *Journal of the American Institute of Planners*, 33, no. 1 (January 1967): 2–10.
10 Caitlin Lempres Brostrom and Richard C. Peters, *The Houses of William Wurster: Frames for Living* (Princeton, NJ: Princeton Architectural Press, 2011).
11 Michael Pyatok, Pyatok Architecture and Urban Design. The firm has done award-winning affordable housing projects for over thirty years.
12 Atul Gawande, "Hellhole," *New Yorker*, March 30, 2009.
13 Frank Gehry played a role in its design, but the basic building behind the simple entry canopy is pure warehouse. Now renamed the Geffen Contemporary at MOCA, Los Angeles, California.

Figure 8.1
Boy in Fountain, Gokseong, South Korea, Noelle E. Jones, photographer

Chapter 8
Does this Place
Support Health?

*Clinical vital signs include heart rate, blood pressure,
temperature, weight, and height. But other, nonmedical
vital signs—such as employment, education, health,
literacy, or safe housing—can also significantly impact
health.[1]*

Robert Wood Johnson Foundation,
To Build a Healthier America, 2014

Can a place make a person sick? It may. A change of zip
code in most American cities can change life expectancy by
five to ten years, even twenty years.[2] Can moving change life
expectancy? Well, not quite so easily. The correlation is there,
but the actual causation includes a wide range of variables,
including safety of all sorts, nutrition, crime, pollution,
employment opportunities, genetics, education, health history,
and access to good medical, dental, and behavioral care.
Recent research correlates public health issues with
geography and investigates the influence on health of a wide
range of environmental factors. The geography of health is
complex.

Settlement Patterns and Health

Historically, settlements were unhealthy places. Early
settlement patterns brought people and animals into close

proximity with their refuse and effluent. Prehistoric settlers typically experienced higher mortality rates than nomads in the same region.[3] Nomadic people could walk away from crowding, contaminated water supply, and lack of sanitation. Nomads had other problems, but the rich ecology of the latrine and the garbage pit added more risk in towns. Diseases that have decimated populations have accompanied urbanization. In times of plague people retreated from cities until they were safe for return.

The wave of rapid city growth with industrialization in the eighteenth and nineteenth centuries led to new sources of disease and mortality. Crowded tenements and slums have long been correlated with a higher incidence of disease. Journalist Jacob Riis documented these problems in nineteenth-century New York tenements.[4] Conditions exposed

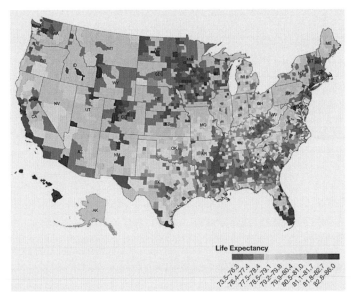

Figure 8.2
Map of Female Life Expectancy in US by County, Kulkarni et al.

by his photography were among the many factors that led to building codes. Access to light and air, sanitary plumbing, fire safety, and structural safety all came under regulation to limit risk of injury, illness, and death. Zoning codes were instituted to restrict inappropriate mixing of uses such as polluting factories and housing.

Yet some of these nineteenth-century tenements, when occupied less densely today by young, middle-class urbanites, may contribute to health. New urbanites have good health care, good education, healthy social networks, good income, and fresh new objects from IKEA. Their lifestyle includes making use of coffee shops, gymnasia, and other community resources as part of their daily pattern of life.

Where a Person Lives Matters

It has been said that, to live a very long life, a person needs to have good genes, strong social connections, and to avoid falling. Cities cannot do much about genes, but they can support opportunities for social connectedness, better diet, and daily exercise. Reducing the risk of falling is more than getting rid of scatter rugs and putting grab-bars in the bathroom. Balance and strength developed over a lifetime can be supported by where people live. Does a neighborhood encourage exercise as part of daily life? Neighborhoods without accessible fresh foods, gathering places, and safe paths for walking and bicycling do not.

Having a fixed abode in itself has come to be a major physical and mental health indicator. Nomadic people in contemporary society face serious risks to health. The North American homeless, in all their variety, are subject to what urban planner Jennifer Wolch has termed "malign neglect."[5] This neglect includes a constellation of factors: poor long-term behavioral health care, poor job prospects (especially for released convicts and the mentally ill), few affordable housing options, and poor health-care options. The places in cities where the homeless congregate and settle, where they are less noticed or hurried on by law enforcement, tend to concentrate social pathologies. Residence on riverbanks, under bridges, in public parks, on vacant lots, and squatting in unoccupied structures may include exposure to pathogens like tuberculosis, behavioral health problems, poor nutrition, poor sanitation, unprotected sex, and increased access to drugs and alcohol, all factors in low life expectancy. Living rough in these places literally makes people sick. In recent years, the Housing First and Rapid Re-Housing movements, among others, have provided stable housing for the homeless as a first step in a support system that aids reintegration in society. It is hard to apply for a job with a riverbank as an address.[6] Harvard professor Matthew Desmond's chronicles of the difficulties of finding and keeping affordable housing in Milwaukee are heartbreaking.[7]

Yet just settling down is not a one-way ticket to a better, healthier life. Where a person lives matters. Epidemiological studies pinpoint less healthy parts of cities, suburbs, and countryside.[8] Investigative work by Jan Schlichtmann[9] in New York and Erin Brockovich[10] in California uncovered carcinogenic pollutants reaching neighborhood water supplies. Certain neighborhoods have very unhealthy crime rates. To what degree does the form of the neighborhood support this threat? As discussed in Chapter 2, neighborhood redesign can reduce the risk of crime. Certain neighborhoods have higher rates of heart disease and diabetes. Research is looking at correlations between food deserts, areas with few outlets for fresh foods, and disease rates. Researchers are continuing to unravel these correlations to understand how the environment impacts physical and mental health.

Sprawl is a Health Risk

Public health experts and urban design experts have written convincingly on the health risks of sprawl.[11] Dense cities with poor infrastructure used to be the culprits. After World War II, developers promoted and people believed that moving to low-density suburbs with light, air, and gardens was the way to achieve healthier lives. Today, evidence suggests health risks are increased in sprawling suburbs.[12] In her *New York Times* column, Jane Brody reported on studies that find "as our drives to work increase in length, health appears to decline." Brody references Swedish evidence that correlates longer commutes with high blood pressure, stress, and heart disease.[13] Significant commute time, hours in many cases, makes it harder to find time to exercise, prepare healthful meals, support family needs, and participate in a rich community and social life. Stay-at-home and working parents in suburban locations spend significant time driving children, who in more compact communities could walk, bicycle, or take buses or trains. Many suburbs lack safe and appealing ways to be a pedestrian, even when destinations are close by. Driving to the gym has come to be the sign of a healthy lifestyle, but is it the most effective way to promote health? Residents of Manhattan are said to weigh six to eight pounds less than their counterparts in the suburbs.

Pediatrician Nooshin Razani reports that increases in childhood obesity and ADHD have paralleled the loss of exercise options for children.[14] The rise of parental supervision for practically everything may have reduced the amount of exercise that children experience on a daily basis, compared to children running wild for hours between school and the evening meal. Author Lenore Skenazy's *Free Range Kids*[15] chronicles what amounts to a new movement to offer kids more chances to escape parental supervision and act on their own. And, yes, learn to manage risks on their own.

Recent literature on urban form describes a migration of low-income people, including many minorities, who are being forced out of cities into the outer suburbs by urban housing costs. They suffer from long and expensive commutes to their jobs, many of which are low-paying service jobs in the increasingly wealthy center city. This is a new form of segregation and can subject minority populations to new health risks.

Today, public health and urban planning professionals are exploring ways to reconfigure suburbs to offer some of the health benefits found in dense urban settlements.[16] Infill projects, like architect Ross Chapin's "pocket neighborhoods," increase density in the suburbs and encourage community. Chapin redevelops single family plots by inserting clusters of houses with porches around shared common space.[17]

In suburbs there is renewed interest in mixed zoning, which includes markets and services within walking or biking distance of home and also brings jobs to the neighborhood. Dannenberg, Frumkin and Jackson argue convincingly for good pedestrian paths that connect to mixed-use centers and other appealing and useful destinations. They do not support a cul-de-sac pattern, because it interrupts connectivity to commercial areas. However, nothing is simple. Advocates for children like environmental design professor Clare Cooper Marcus speak to the benefits of forms like the cul-de-sac, which can support safe play.

An early example of new urbanism, Village Homes in Davis, California, was designed as a sustainable, mixed-use neighborhood with continuous green spaces providing safe pedestrian and bike routes to schools and recreation. These houses, after thirty years, seldom change hands and sell at premium prices.[18]

More recent approaches for transforming residential patterns include transit-oriented development, which increases density at major transit stops. Commercial uses with housing above are adjacent to the transit stop,

Figure 8.3
Transit-oriented development, Oakland, California, Christie Johnson Coffin, photographer

surrounded by lower-density housing within ten-minute walks to the center. These new developments are growing up along existing transit corridors throughout the country, increasing density, making rapid transit practical, and creating walkable neighborhoods with a range of amenities. Even in a metro area as dispersed as Atlanta, Georgia, the Atlanta BeltLine project plans to redevelop a 22-mile railroad corridor that circles the downtown area.[19]

Milieu Therapy

The quality of human and physical environments affects health significantly. Changing places has a therapeutic side. Wanderlust and "the grass is always greener" are phenomena basic to the immigrant and American nature. History, experience, and literature are full of stories about how the journey transforms lives, though sometimes the result may be to better understand the meaning and value of home. Isabel Allende in *Maya's Book* portrays a dramatic, almost magical, behavior change in a teenager who moves from drug, alcohol, and crime problems in the United States to better health on a remote island off the coast of Chile. Although it is largely true that people cannot escape their problems by moving, milieu does affect behavioral health, sometimes almost as dramatically as for Allende's heroine.

Many with drug and chemical dependency problems move out of their home environment for several months, either into residential treatment programs or into different towns. Those who move are more likely to stay clean and sober, even if it takes them several tries to achieve this. Veterans upon their return from the Vietnam War were not expected to escape from chemical dependencies they had acquired. Instead, many succeeded, and this change has been attributed to the therapeutic benefits of home environments compared to conditions of war.

Sunshine and Fresh Air

Places that engage all the senses contribute to a healthy life. This is particularly important for the vision- and hearing-impaired, for whom multisensory design increases independence and integration in the community.[20]

Researchers are investigating how daylight, views, natural ventilation, movement, fragrances, wildlife, art, gardens, and vegetation may be correlated with more effective learning, working, shopping, enjoyment of life, and well-being.[21] Most of what people know about how environment impacts health comes from common sense and experience. These understandings may well be true, but are difficult to prove. People delight in places with sunshine and connections to nature. Many have experienced periods of dim weather, weeks of steady, drizzly rain. When the sun finally comes out, it seems as though everybody has had personality transplants. People are cheerful and outgoing. It is great to be alive.

People enjoy the play of light, especially daylight that is alive and changes during the day. Like other animals, people have biological clocks. Human bodies respond with physical, mental, and behavioral changes to the 24-hour cycle of daylight and darkness. When people behave in ways not in tune with these circadian rhythms, their physiological and emotional functioning can be disturbed. Nightshift workers may have reduced immunity to disease and experience greater risk of accidents and injuries.[22] Regular daily patterns are healthy. Daily, weekly and seasonal changes are invigorating and refreshing.

Fresh air dilutes pathogens that are associated with human disease, making them less likely to cause infection. A study in hospitals suggests that operable windows in patient rooms may improve air quality, compared to air provided by the mechanical ventilation systems.[23] In the Butaro Hospital in Rwanda, each different medical unit is a narrow cross-ventilated wing, not unlike a Nightingale ward, as discussed in Chapter 4. Covered exterior passageways, not interior corridors, link these pavilions, reducing the risk of cross-contamination among units. Air-conditioning systems are costly to build, and expensive and difficult to maintain. In rural Rwanda, frequent electrical service outages are expected, so using natural ventilation and daylighting is often more reliable than mechanical air conditioning and electric lighting.[24]

Even with varied evidence that health and well-being are supported by natural features, designers too often neutralize these factors, eliminating small changes in ambient lighting with electric lighting systems, changes in indoor climate with mechanical heating, cooling, and ventilation systems,

Figure 8.4
Butaro Hospital, Rwanda, MASS Design Group, Iwan Baan, photographer

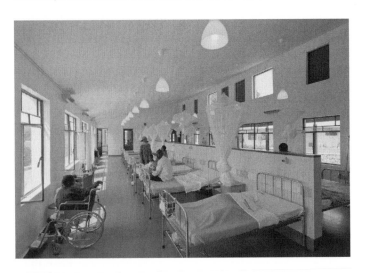

Figure 8.5
Inpatient ward, Butaro Hospital, Rwanda, Iwan Baan, photographer

fragrances with filtration systems, and so forth. The result, aside from possibly being boring, may actually, as in the hospital study described above, carry health risks. People are stimulated by variation and are more alert.

In institutional buildings, large, dense floor plans persist. A surprising percentage of the United States population inhabits artificially "nocturnal" environments, often during the sunniest part of the day. Many contemporary work and shopping places shut out the daylight and view in favor of conditioned, electrically illuminated space.

But things are changing. In many countries in Europe, new buildings provide more daylight. Although hospitals typically feature large compact zones, St. Olav's University Hospital in Trondheim, Norway,[25] did not follow this contemporary practice. Instead, St. Olav's built thin, daylighted, courtyard buildings and retained a grid of city streets, opening the hospital campus to the city. Norwegians value highly the few hours of winter daylight. Scandinavians find that living in the midwinter darkness can be a little like permanent jet lag, not a healthy condition. They research and practice bright light therapy to mitigate seasonal affective disorder in both school children and workers. As the few daylight hours occur during the workday, Scandinavian building codes require effective daylighting in almost all habitable rooms at home and at work, even conference rooms.

Green spaces bring the delight of nature and fresh air to cities. Although quantitative research is scarce, qualitative research is growing for the multifaceted role that green space can play in social, physical, and emotional health.[26] Parks and gardens offer spots for contemplation and provide opportunities for movement and play. Healing gardens are returning as a core feature in hospitals worldwide. Beautiful gardens can offer respite from the stress of being ill or caregiving and be places where solitude and social life can both occur.

Figure 8.6
Hospital Healing Garden, Shenzhen, China, Christie Johnson Coffin, photographer

Because most people in the developed world spend more than 90 percent of their lives indoors,[27] architecture professor Kevin Nute argues for design strategies that bring the experience of weather inside buildings: skylights so people can see and hear the rain, sunshades that protect from heat gain and dapple light, translucent walls showing the movement of wind blowing on bamboo, light reflected off ripples in a nearby pool of water.[28]

Details Matter

Elements of built form like stairs can promote health. Stairs that are visible and welcoming encourage exercise and can contribute to social life. A well-designed stair can become a place where people pause and connect, as well as a stage or a balcony for events.

Even details like the design and location of handwashing sinks matter. Most infections are spread by touch, and

cleaning hands is recognized as the most effective protection against the spread of disease. If designers position sinks strategically, people are more likely to use them. In hospital patient rooms or treatment areas sinks,
if visible at the entry, remind staff and visitors to wash their hands before touching patients and let patients see that staff have, indeed, washed their hands before touching them.

In high-risk areas, like intensive care, the location and the kind of sink needs careful selection. After multiple deaths in an intensive care unit serving organ transplant patients, a Toronto hospital study found that handwashing at sinks placed too close to the patients with gooseneck faucets and shallow basins sprayed water infected with pseudomonas on nearby counters.[29] There are other studies questioning the association between hand hygiene compliance and building plan and design. A sink can provide a significant nudge, encouraging handwashing in hospitals, but cannot force behavior. Peer pressure is needed as well.

Building materiality can affect the health of construction workers as well as occupants. Environmental toxicity can be found in many materials used to construct places. Products today typically do not include lead, asbestos, some fire retardants, and other substances, but new products introduce new potential problems. The introduction of antibiotic countertops and other construction materials may contribute to the development of antibiotic-resistant strains of disease.

Efforts are underway to look not just at the building itself, but also at how it is maintained. Green cleaning methods are emerging. Waxing a floor two to three times may introduce more toxins than a lifetime of environmentally sensitive cleaning. The ability to maintain places with non-toxic cleaning methods may be at least as important as choosing non-toxic building materials in the first place.

Can Designers Do More?

There is a lot more to learn about how to support health and well-being with built form. Today, Florence Nightingale's advice remains the basis of where to start in making healthy places.

> Now, instead of giving medicine, of which you cannot possibly know the exact and proper application, nor all its consequences, would it not be better if you were to persuade and help your poorer neighbors to remove the dung-hill from before the door, to put in a window which opens or an Arnott's ventilator, or to cleanse and lime-wash the cottages?[30]

This chapter focuses on questions designers should ask about making places healthy for people—all places—not just places for medical care. The built environment can support health

Figure 8.7
Village street, India, Christie Johnson Coffin, photographer

and reduce health risks at every scale from sink to regional transportation system. Providing clean water, sanitary sewerage, and hygienic waste disposal has had a greater impact on the longevity of life than almost any medical measure. Around the world many live and work in extremely crowded and unhealthy settlements like favelas in Rio or the slums in Mumbai or Lagos where basic infrastructure is seriously flawed. Designers face tremendous physical, economic, social, and political obstacles in their efforts to contribute to the improvement of global health. How can designers do no harm, removing and mitigating risks to basic health and safety in their work? How can they do better than that and actually promote health and well-being through the design of settlements, cities, transportation, landscapes, neighborhoods, buildings, and rooms?

Notes

1   Robert Wood Johnson Foundation, *To Build a Healthier America,* 2014. Available online at: www.rwjf.org.
2   The Robert Wood Johnson Foundation website gives a life expectancy for any zip code in the United States. Retrieved August 26, 2016 at: www.rwjf.org/en/library/interactives/whereyouliveaffectshowlongyoulive.html.
3   Lawrence J. Angel, "Health as a Crucial Factor in the Changes from Hunting to Developed Farming in the Eastern Mediterranean," in *Paleopathology at the Origins of Agriculture,* ed. Mark N. Cohen and George J. Armelagos (New York: Academic Press, 1984), 51–73.
4   Jacob Riis, *How the Other Half Lives* (New York: Charles Scribner's Sons, 1890). Edited with an introduction by David Leviatin. Boston: Bedford/St. Martin's, 1996.
5   Jennifer R. Wolch and Michael J. Dear. *Malign Neglect: Homelessness in an American City* (San Francisco, CA: Jossey-Bass, 1994).
6   Housing First and Rapid Re-Housing are two movements that provide housing for the homeless as a first step toward reintegrating the homeless in society.
7   Matthew Desmond, *Evicted* (New York: Crown, 2016).
8   The Institute for Health Metrics and Evaluation is a research institute affiliated with the University of Washington. Epidemiological studies can be found on their website: www.healthdata.org/ The map shown is figure 1(a) from the article "Falling Behind: Life Expectancy in US Counties from 2000 to 2007 in an International Context," Sandeep C. Kulkarni, Alison Levin-Rector, Majid Ezzati, and Christopher J. L. Murray, *Population Health Metrics,* 9 (2011):16, doi: 10.1186/1478-7954-91-6.

9   Schlichtmann's work was the documented in Jonathan Harr's book *A Civil Action* (New York: Random House, 1995) and a movie by the same name directed by Steven Zaillian, 1999.

10 Erin Brockovich's work has been widely documented, including in the eponymous movie *Erin Brockovich*, directed by Steven Soderbergh, 2000.

11 Howard Frumkin, Lawrence Frank, and Richard Jackson, *Urban Sprawl and Public Health: Designing, Planning, and Building for Healthy Communities* (Washington, DC: Island Press, 2004) and Andrew L. Dannenberg, Howard Frumkin, and Richard J. Jackson (Eds.) *Making Healthy Places* (Washington, DC: Island Press, 2011).

12 Dannenberg et al., *Making Healthy Places.*

13 Jane E. Brody, "Commuting's Hidden Cost," *New York Times*, October 29, 2013.

14 Nooshin Razani et al., "Neighborhood Characteristics and ADHD: Results of a National Study," *Journal of Attention Disorders*, 19, no. 9 (September 2015): 731–740. doi: 10.1177/1087054714542002; and Nooshin Razani and June M. Tester, "Childhood Obesity and the Built Environment," *Pediatric Annals*, 39, no. 3 (March 2010): 133–139. doi: 10.3928/00904481-20100223-04.

15 Lenore Skenazy, *Free Range Kids: How to Raise Safe, Self-Reliant Children (Without Going Nuts with Worry)* (Hoboken, NJ: Jossey-Bass, 2010). Website: www.freerangekids.com.

16 Ellen Dunham-Jones and June Williamson, *Retrofitting Suburbia* (Hoboken, NJ: Wiley, 2011).

17 Ross Chapin, *Pocket Neighborhoods, Creating Small-Scale Community in a Large-Scale World* (New Town, CT: Taunton Press, 2011).

18 Mark Francis, "Village Homes: A Study in Community Design," *Landscape Journal*, 21, nos. 1–2 (2002). Retrieved August 26, 2016 at: http://lda.ucdavis.edu/people/websites/francis/vh.pdf. Village Homes, Davis, California (architect/developers, Michael and Judy Corbett, built 1973–1982).

19 See the website: http://beltline.org/about/the-atlanta-beltline-project/atlanta-beltline-overview.

20 Christopher Downey, architect, Architecture for the Blind, "Design with the Blind in Mind," TEDCity 2.0 (October 2013). Retrieved August 26, 2016 at: www.ted.com/talks/chris_downey_design_with_the_blind_in_mind?language=en.

21 Marc Schweitzer, Laura Gilpin, and Susan Frampton, "Healing Spaces: Elements of Environmental Design that Make an Impact on Health," *Journal of Alternative and Complementary Medicine*, 10, Suppl. 1 (2004): S71–S83, 79.

22 The National Institute for Occupational Safety and Health (NIOSH) has studied shiftwork, detailing safety and health risks. Rotating shifts offer special risks as it takes weeks to adjust to a new schedule and function at full capacity. Sleep deprivation plays a role in many of the risks. Retrieved August 26, 2016 at: www.cdc.gov/niosh/topics/workschedules/default.html.

23 Steven W. Kembel et al., "Architectural Design Influences the Diversity and Structure of the Built Environment Microbiome," *ISME Journal*, 6 (2012): 1467–1479. Retrieved August 26, 2016 at: www.nature.com/ismej/journal/v6/n8/full/ismej2011211a.html.

24 MASS Design Group with Partners in Health and the Rwandan Ministry of Health, National. Butaro Hospital, Butaro, Burera, Northern Province, Rwanda, 2011, described in *Empowering Architecture: The Butaro Hospital, Rwanda* by the MASS Design Group (Boston, MA: MASS Design Group, 2011), 70.

25 NSW A+P, John Arne Bjerknes, Asrtad Arkitekter, Niels Torp, and Frisk Arkitekter, St. Olaf's Hospital, Trondheim, Norway, 2009.

26 Clare Cooper Marcus and Marnie Barnes (Eds.), *Healing Gardens: Therapeutic Benefits and Design Recommendations* (Hoboken, NJ: Wiley, 1999); and Clare Cooper Marcus and Naomi Sachs, *Therapeutic Landscapes: An Evidence-Based Approach to Designing Healing Gardens and Restorative Outdoor Spaces* (Hoboken, NJ: Wiley, 2013).

27 Jessica Green, "Are We Filtering the Wrong Microbes?" TedGlobal 2011. Retrieved August 26, 2016 at: www.ted.com/talks/jessica_green_good_germs_ make_healthy_buildings?language=en.

28 Kevin Nute, *Vital: Using the Weather to Bring Buildings and Sustainability to Life* (Austin, TX: TBD Publishing Ibook, 2014) and website: www.vitalarchitecture.org.

29 "Sink, the Culprit Behind Infection Outbreak," *Spotlight on Prevention* (December 2008). Retrieved August 26, 2016 at: hospitalacquiredinfections.blogspot.it/2008/ 12/sink-culprit-behind-infection-outbreak.html.

30 Florence Nightingale, *Notes on Nursing: What it Is, and What it Is Not* (Kindle Locations 1668–1670). First published in 1859.

Figure 9.1
Seattle Bicycles, Jerry Finrow, photographer

Chapter 9
What Makes this
Place Sustainable?

All change is not growth, as all movement is not forward.[1]

Ellen Glasgow

sus·tain·able adjective \sə-'stā-nə-bəl
: able to be used without being completely used up or destroyed
: involving methods that do not completely use up or destroy natural resources
: able to last or continue for a long time.[2]

Merriam-Webster Dictionary

Sustainability starts with people. Technology is often the first place people look, but social and personal practices are at the core of sustainability. Can people change their habits and use fewer non-renewable resources? Can people use built form more frugally? Can places adapt to change? Sustainability is supported by places that accommodate changing uses over time and allow for individual control. Can people make socially durable places that their grandchildren will enjoy?

Everyone has been exhorted to recycle, reuse, and reduce. People are nagged daily to change their habits. The question is why aren't they doing it more completely? Why is change happening so slowly? Humans are, it seems, comfortable in their current habits and habits are hard to change.

Unexpected Effects

Popular ideas about sustainability do not take into account inclusive lifecycle costs. Is it more sustainable, for example, to reclaim an industrial wooden floor that may contain toxic chemicals or replace it with bamboo flooring that may have been unsustainably harvested? A professor of sustainable design and planning, Pliny Fisk III, has been arguing for years for adoption of lifecycle-based protocols for evaluating choices in the built environment.[3] He encourages thinking about all the resources needed to mine, grow, transport, manufacture, transport again, store, assemble, install, heat, cool, ventilate, illuminate, maintain, demolish, transport again, remanufacture, repurpose, recycle, and ultimately commit to landfill. Costs fluctuate and are difficult to pin down. Lifecycle costs will be imperfectly calculated.

Sometimes a new technology will solve problems, but all too often people end up consuming more products, transportation, and energy, even in the interests of reducing their carbon footprints. *New Yorker* writer David Owen describes our habit of making choices that give the illusion of sustainability. For example, airplanes use fuel more efficiently today, but people fly more. As he says: "We tend to think, as we ponder strategies for overcoming various environmental difficulties, that technological innovation is a purely benign force. But problems innovate, too—and, usually, they have better funding."[4]

There is a consumer twist to environmentalism that has resulted in a broad range of beautiful products marketed under green labels. Green design enthusiasts remodel perfectly functional buildings to add these green products, which, of course, add to carbon loading. Americans love to shop and consume, and green products are no exception, but wouldn't it be better to consume less? Americans also consume large quantities of space, as discussed in Chapter 4. Some aspire to larger and larger houses, but can a 1,000-square meter (10,000-square foot) house ever be really sustainable?

Unsustainable Transportation Habits

The transportation choices that people make may undermine the overarching goal of sustaining human life. In North America and Europe, most people drive and fly more than they walk and bicycle. Many assume that rural and suburban locations are more sustainable than urban locations, but doing the math can reveal otherwise. Owen's frequently read *New Yorker* article "Green Manhattan"[5] compares Manhattan with semi-rural, suburban Connecticut. When he moved from Manhattan to Connecticut, Owen's energy bill grew by a factor of more than seven. His evaluation of the energy impact of his family's semi-rural lifestyle versus earlier years in Manhattan provides a useful summary of items to include in calculating energy and resource use. His Manhattan apartment had only two of its six sides exposed to weather, proximity to schools, shops, and workplaces, and good public transport options. His family practiced energy conservation habits there not possible in Connecticut. His Connecticut house was free-standing—with weather exposure on five sides—four exterior walls, a roof and a foundation on the earth. There were few walkable destinations, and public transportation was sparse. The family went from being carless to using three cars that clocked 30,000 miles per year, mostly on local trips. Owen speculates that, if Manhattan residents were housed to meet the semi-rural standards of his town, they would occupy six New England states, plus New Jersey and Delaware, and do considerable ecological damage in the process.

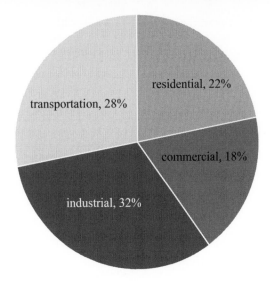

Figure 9.2
Energy use in the United States, 2011, US Energy Information Administration

Nationwide transportation energy costs rival industrial energy costs, averaging about 28 percent of all energy use in 2014, about 30 percent more than residential usage.[6] More efficient transportation is not always sought or even practical. Private vehicles are the only economic alternative in most American neighborhoods. A hybrid car that uses 50 percent less gas may help, although it may encourage more driving and the lifecycle costs of the battery tend to cancel the benefits. Using a car longer may reduce the carbon load more.

Transport habits, tied up as they are with the necessity, convenience, and prestige of private cars, often do not represent sustainable behavior. It is commonly thought that buses or light rail will work at densities of at least thirty dwellings per acre in the area near transit stations. This density is rare in American towns and cities.[7] Americans are in the habit of driving and at present have few options.

What Makes this Place Sustainable?

Bicycle and pedestrian paths can extend sustainable transport options. Bicycle lanes, many of them separated from vehicles and pedestrians, have multiplied in recent years, and more are needed to increase the safety and pleasure of bicycling. In Copenhagen, 45 percent commute by bicycle for part of their work week. Safe bicycle lanes and a fairly flat terrain help make this practical.[8] As a bonus, bicycles cost less. In addition a splurge might mean a $3,000 bicycle, not a $30,000 car. And well-maintained bicycles last longer and will be easier to recycle when they finally wear out.

Sharing as a Sustainability Strategy

In a class exercise, architecture students were asked to propose innovative strategies for reducing energy use. Students started with their most recent energy bills and analyzed how the kilowatts and therms of natural gas were used. They proposed many things like fixing the cracks in their windows, buying sweaters, reducing the hot water temperature, and installing energy-efficient refrigerators. The most effective strategy by far was one student's proposal to recruit a roommate. This cut his energy bill almost in half. This simple lesson is often ignored.

With respect to the issue of too many cars and too much driving, new forms of sharing are emerging. Urban car-sharing systems can provide a standard sedan, a pickup truck for hauling, or a luxury car for a posh night out when needed, without the bother of home parking, repairs, and other issues. Self-driving cars are in the works that may soon offer door-to-door service. New urban bicycle-sharing systems allow a person to pick up a bicycle on the spur of the moment for an errand, a commute, or just for fun. In Barcelona, many bicycle down the hill to work in the morning and take the bus home. The bicycle-sharing service obligingly trucks the bikes back up the hill for morning use the next day. Parking costs and center city tolls are proving to be effective incentives to discourage people from driving. Some urbanites are changing their patterns and do not own cars.

Other forms of sharing are appearing. Home rentals for vacation stays are proliferating. New taxi systems use private cars linked to computer management systems that locate, assign, track, and bill for rides. Traditional hotels and taxis are in the newspaper daily, protesting with complaints that range from unfair licensing fees, insurance, taxes, safety standards, to the cherry-picking of customers. Neighbors are outraged that a next-door home is regularly filled with vacationers, who lack commitment to community norms. These are real concerns, but systemic disruption is underway. Resource sharing has the potential to offer major benefits for environmental stewardship.

Frugal Planning Strategies

Making places that consume less, while fulfilling their purposes is a critical goal of sustainable design. Seven frugal planning strategies are presented in this section that use, as an example, science laboratories, a technically complex and expensive building type that consumes more energy than almost any other. While the impact of these strategies may be more dramatic for laboratories, they give a framework for reducing capital costs and ongoing energy and maintenance costs for a wide range of other places as well.[9]

One: Smaller is greener. The former United States Secretary of Energy, Steven Chu, has said of the laboratories where his Nobel Prize work was done that the "cramped labs and office cubicles forced us to interact with each other and follow each other's progress."[10] Cramped labs in Chu's terms can positively affect the quality of science. People say

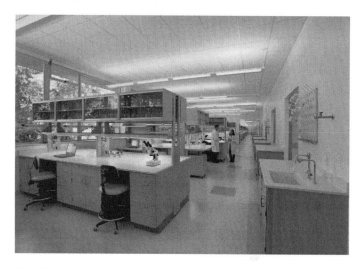

Figure 9.3
Grain Genetics Laboratory, The Design Partnership, architects, Chelsea Olsen, photographer

that the best laboratories are crowded. Are they crowded because they are doing great work, or does the crowding help support great work? Or both? There is no easy way to answer this question. Some laboratories do not look crowded and are reserving space for when that next grant comes in. Many could accommodate additional scientists and students. The overall area of a lab is a key indicator of first costs, maintenance costs, energy costs, and the prestige of the lead scientists and their institutions.

This issue arises in hospital design as well. In the documentary film *Code Black*,[11] the old hospital emergency department seems impossibly crowded and chaotic. In the new hospital, the emergency department is so large that it looks as if no one is home. Remembering the collaboration in the old hospital, the emergency residents rearrange a portion of the new space to increase the density of health-care activity and make sure others are nearby.

Two: Cluster similar uses. The inherently collegial nature of science should direct clustering. If it doesn't make sense for the science, it doesn't make sense for the building. In the physical chemistry building at University of California, Santa Barbara, the designers mechanically cooled only the laboratories and not the offices, which have operable windows and ceiling fans. The chemists agreed that on the four days of the year when air conditioning might be necessary, they could do some intensive work in the laboratories or go off to the beach. Clustering functions with similar systems reduces the size of the mechanical air-conditioning system and the length and energy drop of distribution ducts and pipes. Ducts may be half the cost of an air-conditioning system.

Three: Redundancy is waste. Minimize redundancy by sharing specialized equipment and lightly used spaces. This type of sharing requires generosity and cooperation among different lab groups. It can be frustrating and difficult to manage. Incentives and motivations in institutional space use are complex and political. One person's waste may be another person's meeting room.

Four: Use outdoor space more. Few climates lack comfortable seasons. Even climates with very hot summers and cold winters may have shoulder seasons comfortable for gathering outdoors. Extensions of seminar rooms and break rooms can take advantage of the outdoors. In science laboratories, there may be fewer outdoor options, although one suspects that some physics or engineering experiments would not be hurt by a little fresh air. As discussed in Chapter 8, outside air is often of higher quality than indoor air, and time outdoors during the day is healthy and may even contribute to productivity.

In tropical climates, using shaded outdoor places can reduce construction costs significantly. Colleagues in El Salvador use their outdoor conference space regularly and have installed large computer monitors for video conferencing and technical presentations. The attached coffee kitchen gives

Figure 9.4
Lobby, Khoo Teck Puat Hospital, Singapore, Christie Johnson Coffin, photographer

access to refreshments during meetings. The main lobby of the KPTH Hospital in Singapore is outdoors in the shade of the building above it. Small glass-enclosed kiosks in this large volume offer flowers and gifts to visitors

Five: Concentrate spaciousness and social activity. Making everything as compact as possible can be grim. Spaciousness and beauty will be valued all the more in contrast. One special, spacious place for a larger group to meet, celebrate, practice yoga, or whatever, can give a boost to any cluster of workers. A pattern from *The Oregon Experiment* would call this place a "hearth,"[12] but it might also be known as a symposium room, a sunroom, a playroom, a dining room or a staff break room. The culture of the laboratory can infuse this space. That famous lab at Cambridge where Watson, Crick, and Franklin did their Nobel work had a pub at the top of the building.

Six: Zone the building to support daily patterns of use. There may only be a few in the lab at odd hours. Delivering good air quality and thermal comfort on demand to the few people tending experiments at odd times of the day or year is essential. Their comfort need not include turning on the whole building full blast. Concentrating people who work at odd hours may both create social bonds and increase off-hours personal safety. Differential heating, ventilating, and air-conditioning settings over the day, week, and year can be a major source of energy savings.

Seven: Design for climate. Developing a habit of using mechanical heating, ventilating, and cooling systems as a backup for passive systems is a more sustainable way of planning building technology. Even in buildings as technical as laboratories, many of the spaces can benefit from daylighting, natural ventilation, and passive heating and cooling techniques. Paying attention to orientation, location of mass and openings, insulation, operable windows and vents, and other passive techniques can minimize the size of mechanical heating and cooling systems and the hours of operation required to provide comfort.

In some places people may reject passive solutions because they think they are old-fashioned and lack prestige. Egyptian architect Hassan Fathy, a pioneer in appropriate technology, designed a housing project with traditional Nubian vaults of local mud that work structurally and thermally in the warm, arid climate of the region. The people for whom the mud housing was designed chose to stay in their existing, metal-roofed houses that become hotboxes in the noonday sun and cold in wintry evenings. These houses were adjacent to ancient tombs, where residents worked guiding tourists.[13] Other factors were more important than thermal comfort.

These seven frugal planning strategies can apply to a wide variety of places. They are low-tech and inexpensive and rely on design thinking and social processes.

Sustainable Construction and Maintenance

Habits that support sustainability involve not just design and use of places but also their construction and maintenance. These practices are deeply ingrained, making change complex. In large buildings and on campuses, there has been a tradition in the United States of maintenance and management engineers who were trained by conservative military instructors, served twenty years in the military, and went on to have civilian careers, managing large buildings like hospitals. Their effective work knowledge came solidly from older best practices and often did not include new ideas like solar cells or ground source heat pumps.

Change to adopt more sustainable building systems is slow but has been spurred by new certification programs and code requirements. The work of the United States Green Building Council (USGBC) is one of the more prominent efforts. Founded in 2003, the USGBC LEED program (Leadership in Energy and Environmental Design) has rapidly become a common standard. This program offers certificates and plaques for projects that meet specific criteria for non-toxic, resource-conserving design: green civil engineering; improved indoor air quality; energy-efficient heating, ventilating, and cooling; renewable energy sourcing; daylighting; environmental mitigation; incentives for using rapid transit and bicycling; and more.

The USGBC leaders have been adept at moving slowly enough to involve a broad spectrum of people in the process: contractors, government officials, architects, designers, building inspectors, engineers, real estate developers, and building managers. They have used strategy in considering what to tackle and what to leave alone. From the beginning, people asked why building size, such as house size, was not an issue. Size is generally a reliable indicator: twice as much building, typically twice as much resource and energy use. The answer was that the building contractors would drop out, if reducing size came to the table. So, at that time LEED gave no credit for building smaller. More than ten years later, LEED credit has evolved, and building size is becoming a factor.

Social processes have a lot of inertia. LEED is a sticker system, something parents know can be effective in influencing children's behavior. Owners, designers, and the public now ask for certifications. Not everyone chooses to execute the paperwork and building commissioning involved in a formal rating, but awareness and concern for sustainability have grown broadly and have improved construction practices. It is common knowledge that meeting the California Building Code for new construction is roughly equivalent to a LEED silver rating.

Construction is a complex social process. Places do not always work as designed, nor are they always built according to plan. Testing by an independent third party after the first year of operation can verify that buildings meet their performance goals in practice and not just in theory.

Sustainability issues do not stop with construction. Habits of maintenance include substances that can threaten ecology, as well as health. The pride that professional cleaners bring to waxing floors, for example, as discussed in Chapter 8, is not always consistent with new, gentler cleaning methods. Professional cleaners are beginning to formulate new cleaning products and protocols, which in turn suggest new approaches to the selection of materials for construction.

People-Friendly Technologies

Well-intentioned technologies can be wasted if people cannot figure out how to use them or find them in conflict with other needs. In a school, passive cooling vents near the floor were never opened, because that location proved the perfect place to stack supplies. Complex home thermostats that offer sophisticated choices are often used as on/off switches. Simpler is often more effective.

Environmental control systems are becoming both more sophisticated and easier to use. Early versions of building management systems were often complicated, and did not play well with other proprietary systems. Commercial management systems need expert operation and may not be friendly to building occupants' needs. Building management, responsible for controlling comfort, may encase thermostats out of reach in clear plastic boxes. A physics professor once explained that this provides a small, but helpful, shelf on which to place either a cup of ice water or a cup of hot water to delude the thermostat into thinking the space was too cold, or too hot—an imprecise control but a personal control nonetheless.

One new system allows office workers to tell the heating and cooling system when they are too hot or too cold, and then, the system adjusts, averaging several responses where appropriate. The system works directly with human needs, not theoretical comfort levels. People love the power and it saves energy. Rosa Parks Elementary School[14] has a switch in each classroom to bypass the computer program for one hour at a time, meeting the unpredictable individual classroom need for more heat without disabling energy saving management. Using parts of the school after hours is practical, because the expense of heating up the whole building is not an issue. Air-conditioning specialists, as discussed in Chapter 7, often insist that windows must be fixed for their systems to work efficiently. Fortunately, new, sustainable, user-friendly technologies include switches that turn off the heating and air conditioning, when the window is opened.

Reusing Places

Recycling places retains the embodied energy of existing buildings and brings continuity to human experience. Despite this, people often choose to build new buildings without considering the option of renovation. Typical studio assignments in design schools are for new projects. Building new can make a statement about a person's or an institution's values and can confer prestige. And renovation can be more expensive. The nature of the original construction can hold surprises. The need for special products and constant problem solving may slow building and add costs.

Preserving places adds warmth, texture, and history to the environment, which may be hard to achieve with new structures. Every town and country has its examples: famous buildings like London's Tate Modern, a power station converted to a modern art museum; Portland's Weiden-Kennedy building, a warehouse converted into an advertising agency; hotels converted into low-income single-occupancy housing; or Wisconsin's Oconomowoc Middle School, converted into loft-style apartments for working families.[15]

The legal, social, and political layers of preservation and development are complex and can sometimes conflict. Population growth, migrations, and unforeseen circumstances may require new construction. The challenge for a sustainable future is how to shift the balance from the current paradigm, where the first assumption is to build new, to one that considers historic preservation, adaptive reuse, and new construction all as viable options.

Durable Places

Sustainability is supported best by places that accommodate changing human uses, places that house people and functions so gracefully that renovation is seldom needed except to repair and fine-tune. What makes a building durable in this way? What can be learned from places that have survived and been reused by different groups of people over time? Places that are useful tools have "good bones" and are generous and adaptable, as described in Chapter 7. Warehouses and Victorian houses have had many lives, as people have modified them to meet new and changing needs. Other places have endured because of their special beauty. People want to preserve them and reuse them for the richness and meaning they bring. In studies of contemporary buildings with cutting-edge sustainable technologies, building scientists Bill Bordass and Adrian Leaman describe a "forgiveness factor." They found that in places people liked, they tended to ignore and forgive elements that were not really working.[16]

Heelis,[17] the National Trust's new headquarters in Swindon, United Kingdom, demonstrates building sustainability in several ways. First, the National Trust decided to vacate its offices in London and use its resources to build in the old industrial community of Swindon, bringing jobs and construction to a blighted area. Second, they preserved the industrial buildings in the context. Third, they inserted a new building for offices to demonstrate contemporary sustainable technologies. This building is a large block with a grid of daylighted atrium spaces and exterior courtyards, which become gathering places. The atriums and courtyards ensure that all workers have desks with access to daylight, natural ventilation, and views of nature. The energy load for electric lighting and mechanical ventilation systems is reduced. At the same time, rooftop photovoltaics collect solar energy and shade north-facing

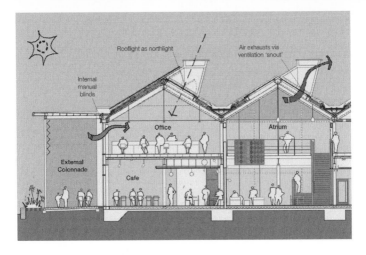

Figure 9.5
Heelis cross section, Swindon, United Kingdom, Feilden Clegg Bradley Studios

Figure 9.6
Heelis entry colonnade, Donald Corner, photographer

Figure 9.7
Heelis work space, Dennis Gilbert, photographer

skylights that also act as ventilation snouts. Attractive wood finishes and art reflect the mission of the organization: to protect historic properties for public use now and in the future. The places that the National Trust stewards have demonstrated their durability. How durable will Heelis be?

Notes

1 Widely attributed to Ellen Glasgow.
2 *Merriam-Webster Dictionary*. Retrieved August 27, 2016 at: www.merriam-webster.com/dictionary/sustainability.
3 Center for Maximum Potential Building Systems, *Center for Maximum Potential Building Systems: 35 Years of Serious Commotion* (Austin, TX: CMPBS, 2010)
4 David Owen, *The Conundrum: How Scientific Innovation, Increased Efficiency, and Good Intentions Can Make our Energy and Climate Problems Worse* (New York: Riverhead Books, 2011), 33.
5 David Owen, "Green Manhattan," *New Yorker*, October 18, 2004, 111ff.

6   US Energy Information Administration, "Energy Use Sector Shares of Total Consumption." Retrieved August 27, 2016 at: www.eia.gov/totalenergy/data/annual/pdf/sec2.pdf.

7   Robert Cervero and Erick Guerra, "Urban Densities and Transit: A Multi-Dimensional Perspective," UC Berkeley Center for Future Urban Transport, 2011. Working Paper UCB-ITS-VWP-2011-6.

8   The Cycling Embassy of Denmark keeps detailed statistics on bicycle use. Retrieved August 27, 2016 at: www.cycling-embassy.dk/facts-about-cycling-in-denmark/statistics.

9   Christie Johnson Coffin, "Seven Frugal Planning Concepts," Labs 21 International Institute for Sustainable Laboratories, Webinar, 2010.

10 Secretary of Energy Steven Chu, quoted in the *New York Times*, July 20, 2011.

11 Ryan McGarry, *Code Black*, 2013, documentary film set in the emergency department at Los Angeles County Hospital.

12 Christopher Alexander et al., "Department Hearth," *The Oregon Experiment* (New York: Oxford University Press, 1975), 131.

13 Hassan Fathy, *Architecture for the Poor* (Chicago: University of Chicago, 1973). Original publication 1969 in Cairo.

14 Ratcliff Architects, Rosa Parks Elementary School, Berkeley, CA, 1998.

15 "'Preservation's Best of 2014' Awards," National Trust for Historic Preservation, March 4, 2015. Retrieved August 27, 2016 at: www.preservationnation.org/who-we-are/press-center/press-releases/2015/preservations-best-of-2014.html.

16 Adrian Leaman and Bill Bordass, "Are Users More Tolerant of 'Green' Buildings?" *Building Research & Information*, 35, no. 6 (2007): 662–673.

17 Feilden Clegg Bradley Studios, Heelis, National Trust Headquarters Building, Swindon, United Kingdom, 2005.

Chapter 10
Who Likes this Place?

I like this place. And willingly could waste my time in it.[1]
William Shakespeare, As You Like It

Liking is a controversial metric. Individuals see places differently. They experience places through their senses, use, memories, and associations. Pleasant or dramatic experiences color people's preferences for place. Human penchants can be rational and emotional, personal and cultural, style-driven and idiosyncratic. Universal preferences lack convincing proof. Design experts' aesthetic judgments may differ from other members of the community, but even experts can disagree. Creating places that everyone will like in every circumstance may not be possible. However, bringing delight and increasing meaning remain at the core of what designers try to do when making places for people.

Creating places with beauty and vitality is challenging. Here is one story about liking:

One of my freshman year writing exercises was severely downgraded because I expressed a liking for the Carpenter Center by Le Corbusier.[2] It may have been a lousy essay, but I read the comments as a criticism of my taste. I was ecstatically in love with the building. It was magical; at least that is how I remember it. I recall literally hugging it to demonstrate to a friend

Figure 10.1 *(facing page)*
Carpenter Center, Le Corbusier, architect, Donald Corner, photographer

my attachment. The fact that Le Corbusier was famous called the building to my attention, but it was only one factor in my liking. It was different from any building that I had ever experienced. More alive. A ramp laced several levels together. The use of transparency and light enchanted. Modular windows created intriguing patterns of light that moved through space over the day.

Later I worked in its studios and attended lectures in the building. Creature comforts were lacking; students froze their feet on the uninsulated, suspended slab, as they struggled on with their Bauhaus training exercises. Yet I continued to love this beautiful, impractical building, which gave me a whole new idea of how to think poetically about space.[3]

Personal, Social, and Cultural Likes

An excited design student, a new place, unusual forms, experiential pleasures—all are factors in the story above. Most likes are deeply embedded in people's social and cultural contexts. Think for a moment about how food preferences develop. There has been significant research showing that very few food preferences, except those like lactose intolerance and seafood allergies, relate to genetic differences. Most food preferences appear to be acquired and culturally influenced. Infants, it is thought, can develop likes and dislikes for almost any food on the planet. Infants will even eat dirt. People develop revulsions to specific foods, like deep-fried silkworm larvae or pork, without any specific biological basis. Often these preferences and aversions are logical in a cultural context, such as disliking pork in the desert and disliking beef in India.[4] Many preferences are acquired in childhood, yet people can also acquire them later on. After seven or eight experiences with a new food, liking can often develop. Most parents employ this knowledge when socializing children to new foods. Dislikes can be quite precise and strong; many Americans prefer not to eat sea cucumbers, for example, though they are wholesome food and delicacies in China.

Comparable processes of acculturation are at work when people develop likes and dislikes for places. Humans have similarly strong likes or antipathies to specific attributes of environments. A place can influence where a person chooses to spend his or her time through a range of qualities. A place can also trigger avoidance.

Often people like places they associate with good memories: a grandparent's house and yard, where one played; a foreign capital visited; a favorite friend's house, where meals were shared; a challenging wilderness trail; a spot in the community where friendly people hung out; or a college, where one studied and found life-long friends. Designers and their clients often seek to replicate, in part or in whole, favorite well-remembered places. The social success of a place may trump comfort or functionality. A person may return to a happily remembered place and be struck by how small and dumpy it is. Architect Peter Zumthor describes being disappointed when revisiting a niche in a wall, which he had admired. At the same time he realized that the quality he remembered was more important than the place itself in fueling creativity. "This difference between the reality and my memories did not surprise me . . . I am satisfied when I am able to retain a feeling, a strong general impression from which I can later extract details as from a painting, and when I can wonder what it was that triggered the sense of protection, warmth, lightness, or spaciousness that has stayed in my memory."[5]

Who you are affects what you like. Architecture and landscape architecture professor Clare Cooper Marcus has written in *House as a Mirror of Self* that people seek to embody their persona in place and gain nourishment from this process. She describes how "our psychological development is punctuated not only by meaningful emotional relationships with people, but also by close affective ties with a number of significant environments, beginning in childhood."[6] These places inevitably form one basis of an individual's spatial vocabulary. Marcus sometimes asked design students to draw their childhood homes from memory, and a few weeks later to draw their "dream houses." The similarities were striking.[7] Designers need to be aware of their personal partialities, which may unconsciously influence their projects.

Social groupings and status connect with place design and what people like. Marcus writes of how Americans of different socio-economic classes make choices that express their status and their aspirations through their houses and their gardens. Delhi architect Gautam Bhatia, who has written with wry wit of Indian architecture, satirizes particular groups in that society for their preferences.[8] He recounts, "One client of mine, a farmer turned garment exporter, wanted me to recreate Thomas Jefferson's Monticello on a suburban lot."[9] Bhatia clearly advocates a preference for simple local forms and has designed using local brick and energy-saving passive design. Yet stage-set architecture is what some clients like. This is true worldwide, as people like places that by association demonstrate to themselves and to others their position in the world. Many of a community's most revered places also emulate historic models. Is it wrong to like something because of its associations?

People like places that support their work and their social life. Friendly spaces attract. They make one comfortable, keep one safe, provide stimulation, and most importantly, include friends and family with whom a person wants to spend time. People like places that welcome them and increase their self-confidence. Veterans using a new mental health center in Palo Alto have commented on the dignity of this clean, attractive hospital, filled with sunshine.[10] They recognize the respect this place gives them for their service to the country.

For designers evaluating projects, it is particularly important to go beyond "I like this," or "I don't like that." One colleague is famous for telling his design students that they need three reasons for every design decision they make, and only one of them can be "I like it."[11] This is an important skill for designers to develop. When clients express likes and dislikes designers need techniques to glean more precisely what that means.

Experiential Likes

As Zumthor writes, "Our perception is visceral. Reason plays a secondary role."[12] Cultural critic Virginia Postrel expands on this idea: "Aesthetics shows, rather than tells, delights rather than instructs. The effects are immediate, perceptual, and emotional. They are not cognitive, although we may analyze them after the fact."[13] First impressions make a big impact, but increased exposure, study, insight, and reflection can shift preferences, as people's likes and dislikes mature and change over time.

Places, of course, enrich life in a variety of ways. Photographs convey only part of the effect. For example, the beauty of Japanese gardens is only partially communicated by photographs. Visible beauty is only one way to describe why people like these gardens. Liking involves all the senses. Strolling through a garden in Kyoto includes the kinetic delight of walking and experiencing light, vista, color, fragrance, texture, and sound. Enclosed spaces, open spaces, and layering of space further enrich this experience. People often choose to visit and revisit these places of special beauty.

Figure 10.2
Kyoto Garden, Howard Davis, photographer

Recent experience with Christopher Downey, a blind architect, illustrates the significance of multisensory experience. Consulting with an architecture firm on a major rehabilitation center, he enlarged the designers' understanding of what makes good places. The designers began to think more clearly in terms of liking a building acoustically, thermally, kinetically, even through odors and fragrances. Downey talked about being warmed, as he passed sunny windows, enjoying the knowledge of where he was. Again, liking is not all visual. That spot with the nice breeze on a hot day is beautiful. Universal delight—not just universal access.[14]

How will fragrances affect a place? Some restaurateurs pipe the smell of baked bread to the sidewalk to signal to passers-by that this is a welcoming place. What about sound? Northern Californian restaurant designer Pat Kuleto was heard saying that everyone wants to find a quiet restaurant, but no one goes there. The sociable noise of a successful restaurant is a big part of what makes it successful.[15] What about temperature? Classic movie theaters pumped cooled air onto the summer sidewalk to draw people in. In Italy in the summer, businesses sometimes spray mist at the entry to entice. So many ways to like a place . . . or not.

Timeless or Transient?

Some places, like the gardens of Kyoto, the Pantheon in Rome, the Chrysler Building in New York, achieve iconic stature for their beauty. People from the culture in which they were created and countless visitors from all around the globe appreciate them. From philosopher Plato to architect Christopher Alexander, who writes of the "timeless"[16] qualities of beauty, there are arguments that "true" beauty is not fleeting or transient. Achieving beauty remains a primary motivation for designers, however difficult it is to attain.

At the same time, there is no doubt that human predilections for built form are subject to fashionable trends. Looking through design journals, one sees definite preferences decade by decade. Urban and architectural historians study aesthetics, and designers learn from their thinking. They have identified superior exemplars of beauty for their proportions, their forms, their craftsmanship, their meaning. Often they focus on places that have been prototypical in history, embodying ideas that have endured, been admired, and been copied over the generations. What value should people give to expert liking? These historians work hard, think a lot, and revisit places multiple times— inspiring others to look more carefully and formulate their own preferences more thoughtfully.

Thinkers like Vitruvius, Alberti, Ruskin, and Corbusier, and more recently Bachelard, Norberg-Schulz, Rasmussen, Alexander, Benedikt, and de Botton have offered insights about how to like places. In each generation new places are identified as worthy of study and new aesthetic canons are formulated.

Decorative elements are particularly controversial. They add depth of meaning, visual interest, celebratory touches— sometimes even humor—to a place. They are often linked to historical periods, but at the same time they contain attributes that transcend particular styles. Throughout history, human tastes have fluctuated from an appreciation for decoration to a desire for simplicity and then back again. Decorations encrusted late medieval buildings. Later, the early Renaissance called for a return to pure forms and unadorned walls. By the Baroque period, designers were breaking all the Renaissance rules, making dramatic spaces with *bel composto*, where architecture, sculpture, decoration, and colored marbles combined for effect. Skipping to the twentieth century, the stripped-down rationalism of the Modern movement rejected the eclecticism of the late nineteenth century. Victorian buildings were thought to be outmoded and fussy, but today, they are again prized. Mid-century Modern design icons have reemerged as worth preserving, after years of destructive remodels by people who wanted something less plain. It seems that expert, aesthetic judgments can be both enriching and varied. Fashion and historical context play a role.

Fashion and tastes can be manipulated. American lawns provide an instructive example. A love of grass may date from when the earliest humans lived in the savannah.[17] People and their animals have regularly trimmed natural grasses and made clearings. However, the desire for the perfect, green lawn became popular after World War II, when, as part of the swords to plowshares movement, explosives factories were converted to manufacture fertilizer. A new standard of lawn was marketed to new suburban homeowners to sell these products.[18] Many Americans now cannot think of a good home without a lush lawn. But times change. In drought-stricken California, many are reverting to older yard fashions, putting in easy-to-grow plants like native sages and imported succulents.

Of course, some likes can be fickle. Fickleness in basic structure is expensive compared to fickleness in paint color, annual plantings, or accessories. But many eccentric places, like architect Sir John Soane's nineteenth-century house museum in London and Simon Rodia's Watts Towers in Los Angeles, become cultural treasures over time.

Getting to Yes

So everything is relative? Or is there a Platonic ideal? Questions to ponder. Designers are tasked with leading the process of making places that many very different people will like and be pleased to use, places that support many goals. Not surprisingly, designers often owe their success in part to their human warmth and ability to listen deeply to their clients, along with real creativity in using both good and perfectly awful suggestions from others. Architect Joseph Esherick used to tell his students that he was never upset if clients did not like a design he presented. He always saw it as an opportunity to design again, something he loved to do.[19] Charles Moore, an architect known for eccentric and exuberant designs, was a great listener. If a client had an idea, even a crazy idea—maybe especially a crazy idea—it landed in the middle of the table and was either an inspiration for the final design or a stepping-stone that helped the design team listen to, take very seriously, and understand the client. Moore's and his coworkers' unusual contract for designing St. Matthew's Episcopal Church in Pacific Palisades, California,[20] required that at least two-thirds of the congregation approve it by vote. The congregation was split. Some wanted a traditional cruciform plan with a nave, while others preferred a church in the

Figure 10.3
St. Matthew's Episcopal Church, Pacific Palisades, California, Moore Ruble Yudell Architects, Timothy Hursley, photographer

round to gather the congregation together. Moore's team did both. The floor plan is fundamentally in the round and the roof is cruciform. The congregation approved the design—87 percent voted yes. St. Matthew's is difficult to photograph, but the place is wonderful in the flesh, the way people experience it. Dialogue can add richness to design.[21]

Commercial developers engage in research to learn what people like. They hold multiple focus groups and analyze the results. People's preferences vary from year to year, and this research provides a long list of likes to be used as a design brief. New developer houses bristle with likable features, such as stainless steel appliances, great rooms, multiple bathrooms, and the latest in countertop material. (Is it quartz this year?) There is no guarantee that checking the boxes in a catalog of likes will result in a warm, likable family home, or any other type of place. In recent years, American housing developers have added many roof gables—Nathaniel Hawthorne is alive and well. Seven or more gables may increase costs without changing anything inside. This building jewelry hints at a spatial playfulness that is not found within. But here lies a common designer "like," a designer's preference for "honesty." Bauhaus training leads many designers to like places that people can read inside and out. Is clarity and simplicity more likable? Or is building adornment desirable to add richness and interest?

Most designers care whether people like their projects and enjoy seeing them appreciated and celebrated in print and online. Some want to push the envelope, provoke people to engage with the places they inhabit. They seek edginess and flirt with dislike to gain attention and make people think. And for the public, as architecture professor Michael Benedikt points out, design, like the fine arts, can open people's eyes. "There are valued times in almost everyone's experience when the world is perceived afresh . . .."[22]

Indeed, some revered buildings were not popular when built. The Eiffel Tower is a famous example.

> Parisians watched in awe & horror as it went up, calling it an "elephant," a "giraffe," a "hulking metal beast crouched on all fours." After it finally opened, it became a huge hit, even with the protesting artists. All except de Maupassant. He hated it so much that he often ate lunch in the tower's second floor restaurant, which was the only point in the city where he couldn't see "this tall skinny pyramid of iron ladders, this giant and disgraceful skeleton.[23]

Controversy has surrounded a surprising range of places, including the Washington Monument, in Washington, DC; the fairytale Neuschwanstein Castle, in Schwangau,

Germany; and Frank Lloyd Wright's Guggenheim Museum, in New York.

Designers are parodied for making expressive (and expensive) forms without paying attention to what building owners and users like. Humorist John Cleese presents a cautionary tale in a Monty Python training video. He impersonates an architect trying to convince his clients that they will love his *abattoir* (slaughterhouse) design. This is a fabulous *abattoir* he claims. The clients respond that they had commissioned him to design a block of flats; he advocates their need for an *abattoir*. The client dismisses him, but in the real world clients are not always so lucky.[24]

Designers can use a variety of methods to stimulate discussion with client groups about what they like. One technique is a variation on the Rorschach test.[25] Designers introduce images of many places and ask clients to say "like" or "don't like" very quickly for each one. Typically the images do not include the designers' own work, giving clients license to like or dislike any image without fear of hurt feelings. These varied images include outlandish places to add humor and to open possibilities. Some images will be disliked by all, ensuring notes of wholehearted consensus. Some will be commonly liked—an image with trees and grass is usually a surefire "like." The results always merit discussion and influence future design decisions.

A more analytic technique that many have found helpful is "choosing by advantages" (CBA).[26] This technique uses a matrix to evaluate design options against the basic goals of a project. People might like one option for its economy, a second for its character, and a third option for its functionality. CBA provides a tool for developing an integrated conversation that focuses on advantages and ways to meet basic goals, while avoiding the pitfall of wasted time discussing all the things that no one likes or wants to do.

Additional methods for bringing together an inclusive conversation without resorting to a plebiscite include focus groups, questionnaires, and formal marketing research techniques. Visiting places together on field trips can be an excellent way for stakeholders to find a common ground. As discussed in Chapter 2, including neighbors' "likes" is important, too. Listening can help a project schedule and make the whole process more pleasant for everyone.

Whose likes will be attended to in designing? The creation of wonderful places that people will really like usually involves many different stakeholders, egos, disciplines and jurisdictions. Years ago, in *Getting to Yes*, negotiation experts Roger Fisher and William Ury[27] offered advice which took good marriage advice to new heights: "Go a little more than halfway and you might meet in the middle."[28] Fisher and Ury's tactical advice emphasizes the value of identifying what people really need rather than assuming that individuals will get everything they want all the time. Most places have compromises; a given person probably won't like everything. Some of the best places harbor interesting contradictions and imperfections. Creating good places is far from easy, requiring the individual creativity of talented designers.

A final question is, does liking matter? The authors believe it does. A place people like during the design phase has a greater chance of being built. Places that are admired and enjoyed may be more likely to be maintained and repaired and to endure. Fashions may change, but places that are truly liked add delight to people's lives and may continue to be useful and meaningful over time. Beauty is sustainable.

Notes

1 William Shakespeare, *As You Like It*, Celia in Act 2: Scene IV: The Forest of Arden.
2 Le Corbusier, Carpenter Center for the Visual Arts, Harvard University, Cambridge, Massachusetts, 1963.

3   Author Christie Johnson Coffin.

4   Marvin Harris, *Cows, Pigs, Wars, and Witches: The Riddles of Culture* (New York: Vintage, 1989), first printed in 1974. Harris, a cultural materialist, offers plausible explanations. Pigs would compete with humans for food and water in the desert. The argument against eating beef in India is more complex and well worth a read.

5   Peter Zumthor, Maureen Oberli-Turner, and Catherine Schelbert, "From a Passion for Things to the Things Themselves," *Thinking Architecture*, (Basel: Birkhäuser, 2nd ed., 2006), 51.

6   Clare Cooper Marcus, *House as a Mirror of Self: Exploring the Deeper Meaning of Home*, 2nd rev. ed. (Berkeley, CA: Conari Press, 1995), 4.

7   Clare Cooper Marcus, "The House as Symbol of the Self," in *Designing for Human Behavior: Architecture and the Behavioral Sciences*, edited by Jon T. Lang (Stroudsburg, PA: Dowden, Hutchinson & Ross, 1974), 145.

8   Gautam Bhatia, *Punjabi Baroque and Other Memories of Architecture* (Penguin Books, 1994).

9   Gautam Bhatia, "New (and Improved?) Delhi," *New York Times*, May 12, 2006.

10 The Design Partnership, architectural team: John Boerger, Christie Johnson Coffin, Marc Schweitzer, Dennis Sullivan, Lakshmi Nair, David Hall, Building 520: Mental Health Center, Veterans Affairs Palo Alto Health Care System, Palo Alto, CA, 2012.

11 Architect and professor Otto Poticha, University of Oregon, heard by author Jenny Young.

12 Peter Zumthor et al., "Does Beauty Have a Form?" *Thinking Architecture*, 77.

13 Virginia Postrel, "The Aesthetic Imperative," *The Substance of Style* (New York:Harper Perennial, 2004), 6.

14 Architect Christopher Downey, Architecture for the Blind, heard by author Christie Johnson Coffin.

15 Restaurant designer Pat Kuleto, heard by author Christie Johnson Coffin.

16 Christopher Alexander, *The Timeless Way of Building*, (New York: Oxford University Press, 1979).

17 Grant Hildebrand, *Origins of Architectural Pleasure* (Berkeley, CA: University of California Press, 1999).

18 Paul Robbins, *Lawn People* (Philadelphia, PA: Temple University Press, 2007). Robbins, an anthropologist, chronicles the history of the lawn.

19 Architect Joseph Esherick, told to Jenny Young, design studio, University of California, Berkeley, spring 1971.

20 Moore, Ruble, Yudell, Architects and Planners, St. Matthew's Episcopal Church, Pacific Palisades, California, 1983.

21 Karen A. Franck and Teresa von Sommaruga Howard, *Design through Dialogue: A Guide for Clients and Architects* (New York: Wiley, 2010).

22 Michael Benedikt, *For an Architecture of Reality* (Santa Fe, NM: Lumen, 1992).

23 "The Eiffel Tower, 10 Notable Buildings People Hated," The Sanity Inspector, Listverse, October 21, 2010. Retrieved August 27, 2016 at: http://listverse.com/2010/10/21/10-notable-buildings-people-hated.

24 Monty Python, "Architects Sketch," Episode 17, *Monty Python's Flying Circus*, recorded September 18, 1970 and originally aired October 20, 1970, filmed as part of John Cleese's business management films series. Retrieved August 27, 2016 at: www.youtube.com/watch?v=DyL5mAqFJds.

25   Author Christie Johnson Coffin learned this technique from Stephen Harby of Moore Ruble Yudell, Architects and Planners, while working together on the University of Oregon science buildings.

26   Jim Suhr, *The Choosing by Advantages Decisionmaking System* (Westport, CT: Praeger, 1999).

27   Roger Fisher, William L. Ury, and Bruce Patton, *Getting to Yes: Negotiating Agreement without Giving In* (Penguin, 2011).

28   Author Christie Johnson Coffin's Aunt Peggy gave this marriage advice.

Figure 11.1
Dilbert, Scott Adams, cartoonist

Chapter 11
What Evidence is there this Place will Work?

Evidence, broadly construed, is anything presented in support of an assertion. This support may be strong or weak. The strongest type of evidence is that which provides direct proof of the truth of an assertion. At the other extreme is evidence that is merely consistent with an assertion but does not rule out other, contradictory assertions, as in circumstantial evidence.[1]

Wikipedia

The evidence is contradictory on how built form affects people's lives. Making places is expensive, and people search for evidence to support design decisions to ensure that what they build will effectively meet their needs and goals. Curiosity about the roles that crowding, daylight, levels of privacy, adjacency, colors, clarity, beauty, and other environmental characteristics play in behavior has led to research. Although the evidence is spotty, it is increasing.

Environmental design research ranges from rigorous social science studies, focusing on a single feature like a view or daylighting, to more prompt and practical investigations, often integrating many features. Design involves orchestrating a huge and motley collection of information and evaluating the many design options in any situation. Design projects provide the opportunity to learn more about the relationships between people and places.

Research Evidence

Evidence about how the environment impacts human behavior lacks precision by the standards of laboratory science. Costs for human subject research are very high. The variables are, well, too variable. Dependent variables are rarely controllable. The chance of *post hoc ergo propter hoc* fallacy (after it, therefore because of it) is likely. Often the best environmental research demonstrates correlation, not causation. Some skepticism is rational.

Some of the earliest documented experiments about how the environment affects people were done at the Western Electric Hawthorne Works in Cicero, Illinois, in the 1920s and 1930s. Researchers questioned whether changing the level of illumination in a factory workshop could improve workers' productivity. In one room, the light was systematically altered, and in another, which served as the control, the light was kept the same. Each room housed about five women workers. Surprisingly, productivity increased in both places, even when the light was dimmed to a level that made seeing the work difficult. The common interpretations of this research are that the workers were more productive when management paid attention to them and when their work environment changed. The observer effect continues to be a concern in research. More experiments followed, and the results are still discussed and disputed decades later. They point to the complexity of proving one-to-one causation between an environmental feature and human behavior. This is not to say that illumination does not impact productivity, but that it depends on many factors: the person, the kind of job, and the kind of light, among others.[2]

Roger Ulrich's frequently cited study, showing the value of windows with views of nature for hospital patients,[3] did not depend on people being watched in an experiment, but relied on six years of existing hospital records. Staff and patients had no reason to anticipate this data would be used in a future study. Ulrich's study compared twenty-three postoperative patients who had bedroom windows with a view of a tree, with a matched group of twenty-three patients with views of a brick wall. All forty-six patients had experienced a single type of routine gall bladder surgery and had no major complications. They ranged in age from seventeen to sixty-nine. They were randomly assigned to rooms, based on availability. Patients who experienced the tree view had a shorter stay in the hospital, took less pain medicine, and had fewer negative and more positive evaluative comments from nurses.

This respected piece of research is widely used as design evidence to support the practice of providing hospital bedrooms with windows and views. Comparing this study to medical studies with data on thousands, even tens of thousands, of people, illustrates the limited nature of many design research efforts. Environmental design research seldom can afford to take into account the fascinating variability of social life. Ulrich's study was based on data commonly gathered by caregivers. Had there been care protocol or staffing changes over the six-year period? Were there gender or ethnic differences? Were there acoustic factors? Was distance from the staff center an issue? Did senior nursing staff prefer to serve patients with view windows? Would this result occur for other types of surgery? Would it occur for patients who had more complex medical needs? Was patient support by their families and friends equivalent? Control for all factors is hard to achieve. And again, was the sample size large enough for generalization?

Having windows with views of nature is a message designers like to hear. They believe it is accurate and it may be. This raises yet another question: Is belief an appropriate word to use when talking about evidence? Designers often work with less than robust information. As psychologist Lance Rips has written "Much of our thinking is about what

might be or must be true, not just what is actually true."[4]
Even with the questions raised above, Ulrich's study and
other supporting studies have affected hospital design.

A very different source of evidence for designers is
A Pattern Language,[5] probably the best-selling architectural
book in history. In this 1977 book, Christopher Alexander,
Sara Ishikawa, Murray Silverstein, and others describe
hypotheses that attempt to make workable connections
between place and social life, connections that people can
use in designing. Compared to Ulrich, who was working with
one hypothesis, *A Pattern Language* contains 253 hypotheses
from the scale of urban design to furnishing the interior of
a house. Compared to Ulrich's research, this evidence varies
in kind and rigor. Some criticize *A Pattern Language* as
"pseudo-science," because the evidence lacks consistent rigor.
However, like good science, the hypotheses are clear, and
the evidence is stated, so it can be criticized or replicated,
and the hypotheses can be affirmed, repudiated, or modified
over time.

Where *A Pattern Language* has sacrificed credibility is in
the firmness with which these social and spatial patterns
are expressed. Patterns say "shall" and "will," not "could"
or "might." Most readers do not even notice that the authors
rated more successful patterns with asterisks. Patterns
with two asterisks describe "a deep and inescapable
property of a well-formed environment,"[6] while patterns
with no asterisks have not succeeded in identifying an
invariant, but can open discussion by "providing at least
one possible way of solving the problem."[7] The concept is
"A" pattern language and not "The" pattern language. The
authors anticipated that others would use the evidence as a
basis for further experiments to produce different forms and
different languages. One of the authors, architect Shlomo
Angel, has said that *A Pattern Language* describes the
"alcovic nature of the universe."[8] Indeed, the patterns in
the book do favor alcoves and other smaller places for

Figure 11.2
A Pattern Language in use

people on the edge of larger places, which are not everyone's cup of tea.

"Site Repair,"[9] discussed in Chapter 3, has two asterisks. This pattern, which argues that each project identify site flaws and repair them, is based on a logical argument rather than research evidence. It rings true. The University of Oregon under its original pattern language-based master plan, *The Oregon Experiment*, adopted it. Not everything that is critical in design can be proved with research.

In contrast, "Accessible Green,"[10] another pattern with two asterisks, is a pattern based on limited research evidence. This pattern advocates parks within three-minutes' walking distance of all houses. It argues that parks farther away are not used. The research cited includes a citizen survey of park use by the Berkeley City Planning Department and a survey of twenty-two people using a Berkeley park. The sample is small, but the method is clear. The experiment can be replicated. At the same time, evidence in isolation is not enough. If a town had parks within 750 feet of every house, what other social and economic goals would be affected?

Perhaps the gold standard of contemporary environment and behavior research is architect Lisa Heschong's research on the effects of daylight on learning in elementary school classrooms. These studies relied on standardized educational test data for third, fourth, and fifth graders, which schools were already collecting, and first-hand analysis of classroom daylighting. Researchers looked for correlations between test scores and quality of daylight in the classroom. Meticulous multivariate analysis compared the effects of fifty or more variables to assess their roles in student performance. Peer review turned up additional variables and research questions, which then were pursued to refine the results. For example, did the star teachers get the naturally illuminated rooms? No, they chose the rooms with other benefits, like larger size or more storage. Heschong concluded, "various window characteristics of classrooms . . . had as much explanatory power in explaining variation in student performance as more traditional educational metrics, such as teacher characteristics, number of computers, or attendance rates."[11] Few environmental research studies approach the rigor of Heschong's team. Her work makes a convincing connection between academic performance and daylight. Heschong's other research has added evidence that daylight adds value for retail sales and office performance.

Pitfalls in Design Research

Evidence in design should be used very carefully. Changes in the environment are often made with imperfect evidence. Here are three examples.

The first example is a hypothesis from the 1960s, when windowless classrooms were promoted with claims that they would curtail vandalism, lower construction costs, reduce energy loss, and minimize student distraction. Many factors supported this idea. Windows were expensive. At the time, most were single-paned and lost energy. Electric light could replace daylighting for needed illumination. Mechanical engineers wanted to eliminate operable windows to control comfort with mechanical systems. Clustering classrooms compactly without windows allowed greater density on constricted sites.

It is hard to trace whether there was any actual evidence to support this widespread practice. National Bureau of Standards researcher Belinda Collins provided an extensive bibliography and summary of available research and concluded that there was little evidence that windows were needed.[12] Heschong's work, of course, came later. Teachers had opinions both for and against windowless classrooms. The distraction issues posed by windows became almost an urban myth in school design with little or no supporting evidence. The premise was controversial at the time.

With new evidence, daylighted classrooms have reemerged as the common standard. Yet, new windowless classrooms are often built as part of hospitals, corporate headquarters, and other places, where the benefits of daylighting may also apply. With new technology in window design and sun-screening devices and new attention to passive heating and cooling, it is possible to improve classroom performance without a significant energy penalty. As discussed in Chapter 8, in northern places, daylight is particularly important during the long winters. Windowless classrooms and conference rooms are not legal in Scandinavia, where work and school coincide with the few winter daylight hours.

The second example highlights a question about research bias. Common wisdom in workplace design says that open offices generate useful informal communication and creativity, make efficient use of space, allow managers to manage in a friendly informal way, and are highly adaptable. In the last one hundred years, employers have tried a variety of open office approaches to improve office layout, often providing rectangular cubicles in a large open plan. Some progressive companies boast that everyone is treated equitably; no one has a private office.

Detailed studies have led to new furnishing systems to support workplace designs. Brilliant office planners and designers like the Schnelle brothers who developed *Bürolandschaft* (office landscaping), Florence Knoll, Robert Probst, and others have spawned new ways to arrange and furnish office space. Strikingly, major furniture manufacturers have paid for most of this office research directly or indirectly.[13] The worldwide embrace of open office and standardized cubicles has provided a rich market for these manufacturers. Cubicle partitions, furnishings, and accessories are typically twice the cost of floor-mounted furniture and require professional help and a medley of proprietary parts to install, move, or use effectively. Conflict of interest? Perhaps.[14]

What are the benefits of open offices in actual practice? The productivity of office workers is hard to measure, but evidence supports problems with concentration and productivity. Researchers measure retention rates, sick days, and absenteeism. These factors are surrogates for actual productivity. Does useful communication actually improve? It is not clear. Is it easier to supervise and control employees? Are employees more effective in large open offices?[15]

There has been significant research within the concept of open office, but rarely does this research address other options. Research has tended to focus on larger aggregations of workers and not on more compartmented approaches. For example, would smaller rooms, accommodating six to eight workers, be more effective? Would four-person offices, eight-person offices, or even private offices work better? The design firm IDEO[16] assigns staff tiny spaces at shared tables in an open zone and provides lockable project rooms for teams of five to ten people, where most of the work gets done. This arrangement supports IDEO's work, which is often patentable or trademarked. Other types of work may thrive in different environments.

Employers often select office furniture systems for their adaptability. But are they adaptable? The discipline imposed by the system can limit rearrangement options and contribute to inefficient use of space, where modules meet the columns, walls, and duct shafts particular to an existing building. Quality of workplace is trumped by furniture limitations. Many of these systems remain in place for decades. Anyone who has tried to reconfigure an office system knows why. They discover the need for a professional crew and multiple, new, costly, proprietary parts, which may be difficult to find for legacy systems. When change is needed, replacement with a new "flexible system" often proves a practical, if expensive, solution. Will the new cubicle systems be easier to adapt? Some contemporary companies are changing to floor-mounted furnishings that any two adults can move without expert help.

Not surprisingly every few years, or at least every decade, new productivity tools in the form of new office systems show up on the market. The *Harvard Business Review* reported on office productivity research to monitor a major change in office layout from a cubicle farm to a more open array with less individually assigned space and more shared collaborative space. The improvements were dramatic: more timely communications, fewer hours lost, better ergonomics, less disruption at smaller desks with more nearby collaboration space, and overall 25 percent less space per person with lower capital and furniture costs.[17] It is a very detailed and well-studied case, but is it applicable in another situation? Again new office furnishing products are on offer at the suggestion of individuals who may profit by the change. The results may be perfectly true, but the source of research is always worth questioning.

The third example of the pitfalls of research is at an urban and regional scale. Communities everywhere are dominated by wide roadways, which have been designed largely to meet fire department requirements and traffic engineering guidelines. Vehicle safety and the maneuvering space needed by firefighting equipment have provided key evidence for these practices. Dedicated bicyclists and pedestrians have continued to walk and cycle on these roadways, often at some risk to their safety, and certainly to the detriment of the quality of the experience. The percentage of land in impermeable paving has raised environmental concerns relating to the growth of heat islands and the reduction of area for replenishing aquifers. Modifying firefighting equipment could minimize pavement requirements.

Figure 11.3
Parklet, Berkeley, California, Jenny Young, photographer

Figure 11.4
Helsinki esplanade, Jerry Finrow, photographer

Danish urban planners Jan Gehl and Birgitte Svarre in *How to Study Public Life* have written about how in these practices "Public life and the interaction between life and space was neglected."[18] This happens as design professionals follow their particular specialties, be it fire protection, streets, drainage, gardens, or buildings. Each piece may be based on its own book of evidence, but the overall life of the community may fall between the cracks. Recently, communities have begun to reclaim streets for other purposes: parklets, bicycle paths, pedestrian zones. Unlike mid-century pedestrian malls that excluded cars and bicycles, Gehl and Svarre and a University of Oregon team in a study called *Rethinking Streets* promote redesigning existing streets to accommodate cars, bicycles, and people.[19] Evidence is beginning to come in not just on safety, but also on making places that support a lively community use of public space.

Design as Inquiry

When people design places, they are making thousands of decisions, and each one of those decisions is a hypothesis. A designer will think, if I make a bench 60 cm (25 inches) wide, people will be able to comfortably sit on it. How does she know that? Is she right? Will she observe the bench in use later and affirm her decision?

In practice, when people are designing, they need to test the relevance of an amazing number of design decisions to the purpose at hand. For some things, like the size of a bench, experienced designers may have internalized the knowledge. They may have first learned it by sitting on benches, measuring the ones that felt comfortable, or they may have asked someone, looked it up on the Internet, or used a reference like *Architectural Graphic Standards*.[20] The research on many of these questions is practical and prompt, occurring many times in a day's work. The results show up directly in design decisions.

The simplest forms of research are conversation, listening, and firsthand observation of how people use a place. Astute designers always hold conversations with clients at the client's residence or workplace, so they can listen but also observe and ask questions about what they observe. It matters who is included in these conversations, as discussed in Chapter 2. When working on a project to bring humane health care to California prisons, the large design team had multiple conversations with prison officials and current expert practitioners in prison design. Missing was a candid exchange of information with prisoners. Also missing were the voices of critics calling for prison reform. The end result was a minor revision of previous prison planning that did not include many lessons learned from successful reform measures in use in other parts of the United States and Europe. Evidence was ignored.

Methods used in environment-behavior research
from peer-reviewed and published to practical and prompt

relevant – reliable – replicable (the three Rs)
using multiple methods to triangulate and confirm hypotheses

Observation *Obtrusive and Non-obtrusive*	Direct Observation • Tracking "a day in a life" • Activity log/blog (people tracking their own behavior over a period of time) • Behavior specimen record (observing one person over a period of time) • Mapping behavior—observing activities—who is doing what—with whom—over time (in person, with photographs, with video) Observation of traces Long-term immersion—ethnography
Questions and Answers *Informal or Structured*	Interviews Focus Groups Questionnaires Surveys Participatory Processes Meetings, Charrettes, Open Houses
Existing data *Records and documents*	Published Research Analysis of Documents
Case studies *Benchmarking*	Documentation and Analysis of Existing Places Visiting Benchmark Buildings

Figure 11.5
Table of research methods

Observing people in places, watching a transplant operation by video, joining a family in preparing a meal, or tracking a factory worker throughout a day gives designers useful information. Direct observation of how people use places needs to take into account how observers may affect the outcome. Recall the Hawthorne experiments. Observation can be intrusive in different degrees, depending on the amount of privacy the activity typically enjoys. Designers can also go undercover to get the inside story, although observing people without their knowledge raises ethical issues. It is important to remember in observing to strive for a representative sample. What happens at other times of the day, or when conditions are different? Spending a day in a wheelchair can give an idea of that experience, but as an expert in designing for people with disabilities pointed out, a day in a wheelchair only touches the surface of what life in a chair is about.

Observation of places even without people present can be informative. Sociologist John Zeisel in his book *Inquiry by Design*[21] describes a process of looking for traces or evidence of human use, to understand how those places have been used or abused over time. In this mode, designers act like archaeologists and investigate: Where have walls been repaired? Where has flooring been worn away? Where have paths been worn in the grass? What features collect graffiti? The list is endless. This is a popular exercise for design students, who create imaginative photo essays that document space use and inform the next designer.

Design teams often seek out benchmark examples. Reading is a first step, but visiting places with clients adds more. On benchmark visits, the whole team observes the use and misuse of built form, documents spaces and activities, listens to residents or users evaluate their experiences in the place, and tries to envision what it would be like to use features of this place. Anecdotal? Yes. Practical? Yes. These field trips expand, enrich, and help decode design conversation. For the assignment to plan a new 550-bed eye hospital in Chennai, the design team and members of the hospital executive group traveled for ten days and visited ten hospitals. This activity gave everyone evidence for what would work and what would not. Everyone started with many ideas, which were refined and clarified by the visits. The visits probably saved much more time than they took, because the team members achieved agreement on many issues before they put pencils to paper and fingers to keyboards.

Many projects provide the opportunity to learn more about the relationship between form and behavior. In one evidence-based project, architects Mardelle McCuskey Shepley and John Boerger researched the incidence of violence in an acute adolescent psychiatric hospital in California. This work made adroit use of existing data, almost a must in minimally funded environmental research, and virtually a necessity in practice. They mapped data that had been consistently gathered by mental health staff over many years, which pinpointed where violent incidents occurred. This research demonstrated that on an adolescent behavioral ward, ambiguous turf, dead-end corridors, and corridors in general tended to be more dangerous than clear and visible areas.[22] With this critical information, Shepley and Boerger avoided these typical venues for violence in their design. Violent incidents were almost eliminated in the new facility.

This example of developing knowledge as part of an architectural commission won a top award the year it was completed. Although robust, this research has not been widely disseminated, as venues for publication are few and practitioners seldom have time to pursue publication of their investigations.

Post-Occupancy Evaluation

Learning from mistakes and successes is how the quality of built form improves. Evaluating new built places after they have been occupied should be a more common part of design practice. Post-occupancy evaluation (POE) can use a range of criteria: the goals of the original program, the desires of current users, or third-party standards. In a POE evaluating two Head Start buildings, criteria included the stability of the program, staff retention, the logic of the building organization, indoor–outdoor connections, and flexibility for furnishing and use.[23] In energy audits, the criteria relate to where and how much various sources of energy are deployed. A really informative POE by a third party will examine multiple criteria. Many university design programs have found this a valuable pursuit.

Designers often speak of completing post-occupancy evaluations, but they are seldom a regular practice. Institutions with large real estate portfolios sometimes do very detailed evaluations, but that proprietary work is seldom shared with competitors or exposed to possible litigants. Builders and designers may never see those studies. The incentive for other owners and designers to perform a POE is the opportunity to build their understanding and knowledge and collect information for future projects.[24] This motivation is weak in the absence of funding and time. Designers are rarely paid for this work, and owners may have little motivation to improve the lot of the next client. Both may have fears that a POE will unearth problems that could result in litigation. Sociologist Galen Cranz argues that POEs can be part of everyday practice. Every POE need not be full-blown research.[25] By working within a simple, consistent research plan, designers can economically conduct interviews and observations, which can over time be assembled into useful evidence and increase knowledge.

Changing Contexts for Design Research

In spite of the difficulties, most designers and planners do include well-researched evidence as part of the design decision-making process. A contemporary design movement, "evidence-based design," urges paying attention to credible environmental research. Led by health-care design architects at the Center for Healthcare Design and Texas A&M University, this effort has become institutionalized and now has a methodology, publications, and a certification program to train and recognize designers devoted to rationality.[26] This approach is modeled after an evidence-based medicine movement, which seeks to promote a more rigorously scientific approach to medical decision-making.[27] Evidence-based medicine is defined as "conscientious, explicit, and judicious use of current best evidence in making decisions about the care of individual patients."[28] In medicine, this means being very critical of intuition and anecdotal evidence, using pharmaceutical products only for purposes justified by research. Understandably, the adoption of evidence-based design has been piecemeal. Well-researched evidence is limited, and artistic intuitions and anecdotal evidence are valued to inspire the creation of unique and wonderful places.

Even if the evidence is useful for today, people change, needs change. Much of the basic research on open offices predated universal use of computers. The open office of today may be the virtual open office that allows workers to complete assignments at the office, at home, in a co-work space, or on a beach in Brazil. Times are changing. It is likely that design will always be an indeterminate process. Designers learn from each project. Their curiosity, research, and growing knowledge increase their ability to understand how to create places that enrich rather than limit human lives, planning for slack as well as fit and delight as well as sober functionality.

Notes

1 Retrieved August 28, 2016 at: https://en.wikipedia.org/wiki/Evidence
2 Jerald Greenberg and Robert A. Baron, "Organizational Behavior: A Historical Overview," *Behavior in Organizations*, 4th ed. (Boston, MA: Allyn & Bacon, 1993), 13–16.
3 Roger S. Ulrich, "View through a Window May Influence Recovery from Surgery," *Science*, 224, no. 4647 (April 27, 1984), 420–421.
4 Lance J. Rips, *Lines of Thought, Central Concepts in Cognitive Psychology*, p. vii, (New York and Oxford, Oxford University Press, 2011).
5 Christopher Alexander et al., *A Pattern Language* (New York: Oxford Press, 1977), xiv.
6 Alexander et al., *Pattern Language*, xiv.
7 Alexander et al., *Pattern Language*, xv.
8 Shlomo Angel in conversation with author Christie Johnson Coffin.
9 Christopher Alexander et al., "104, Site Repair," *A Pattern Language*, 508–512.
10 Christopher Alexander et al., "60, Accessible Green," *A Pattern Language*, 304–309.
11 Lisa Heschong, *Windows and Classrooms: A Study of Student Performance and the Indoor Environment*, California Energy Commission Report, October 2003. Retrieved August 28, 2016 at: www.energy.ca.gov/2003publications/CEC-500-2003-082/CEC-500-2003-082-A-07.PDF; and Lisa Heschong, Roger L. Wright, and Stacie Okura, "Daylighting Impacts on Human Performance in School," *Journal of the Illuminating Engineering Society*, 31, no. 2 (Summer 2002): 101–114.
12 Belinda Collins, National Bureau of Standards. This thorough bibliography, completed in the mid-1960s, is no longer available from the government office.
13 The Schnelle brothers, who developed *Bürolandschaft* (office landscaping), were furniture manufacturers. Florence Knoll, an influential designer, founded Knoll, a furniture company still providing office furniture. Robert Probst worked for Herman Miller. Many who practice interior design for offices make a profit from the sale of these furnishings. Ideas about the value of open office systems may be quite accurate, but many have applied them without questioning their bias.
14 Michael Brill with Stephen T. Margulis, Ellen Konar, and BOSTI, *Using Office Design to Increase Productivity*, 2 vols. (Buffalo, NY: Workplace Productivity, Westinghouse Furniture Systems, 1984). Brill's two-volume work provides a wealth of data on how offices are used, although it predates contemporary use of computers and digital forms of information. Michael Brill, Sue Weidermann, and BOSTI, *Widespread Myths about Workplace Design* (Jasper, IN: Kimball International, 2000) retrieved October 30, 2016 at: http://qz.com/85400/moving-to-open-plan-offices-makes-employees-less-productive-less-happy-and-more-likely-to-get-sick/.
15 Maria Konnikova, "The Open-Office Trap," *New Yorker*, January 7, 2014.
16 Observed by author Christie Johnson Coffin.
17 Laing, Andrew, David Craig, and Alex White, "Vision Statement: High Performance Office Space," *Harvard Business Review*, September 2011.
18 Jan Gehl and Birgitte Svarre, *How to Study Public Life* (Washington, DC: Island Press, 2013). Claire Martin, "Where the Parking Space Becomes a Park," *New York Times*, January 10, 2015. Parklets are a recent phenomenon, transforming

parking spaces into public gathering places for eating and other social purposes. Many websites describe this active movement, such as http://pavementtoparks.org

19 Marc Schlossberg, John Rowell, Dave Amos, Kelly Sanford, *Rethinking Streets* (Eugene, OR: Sustainable Cities Initiative, University of Oregon, 2013).

20 American Institute of Architects and Dennis Hall, *Architectural Graphic Standards*, 16th ed. (Hoboken, NJ: Wiley, 2016).

21 John Zeisel, *Inquiry by Design: Environment/Behavior/Neuroscience in Architecture, Interiors, Landscape, and Planning*, rev. ed. (New York: W. W. Norton, 2006).

22 Mardelle McCuskey Shepley with John Boerger, "Designing a Children's Psychiatric Facility" (Design Partnership: 1989). Privately published research paper.

23 Jenny Young and Anna Liu, *Five Years Later: Lessons Learned from Two Early Childhood Centers*, February 2013.

24 W. F. E. Preiser, H. Z. Rabinowitz, and E. T. White, *Post Occupancy Evaluation* (New York: Van Nostrand Reinhold, 1988). This is a classic reference.

25 Galen Cranz, Amy Taylor, and Anne-Marie Broudehoux, "Community and Complexity on Campus and How to Grow a Business School," *Places* 11, no. 1 (1997), 51.

26 D. Kirk Hamilton and Mardelle McCuskey Shepley, *Design for Critical Care: An Evidence Based Approach* (London and New York: Routledge, 2009).

27 EDAC offers training and certification see: www.healthdesign.org/edac.

28 D. L. Sackett et al., "Evidence Based Medicine: What it Is and what it Isn't," *British Medical Journal*, 312 (January 13, 1996): 71–72.

Chapter 12
Does this Place Foster Social Equity?

No one sets out to ignore equity, but the way we frame issues of causality and response typically fail to give it due consideration. Equity is less the proverbial elephant in the room than the elephant lumbering around a maze of screens dividing that room into a series of confined spaces.[1]

Paul Farmer

Social equity is a global concern. People live in poverty and in wealth. These differences are often extreme, with many living and working in places that do not provide basic shelter from weather, war, domestic violence, hunger, and disease. Many people have limited access to opportunities that would assist them in improving their own lot. At the same time, others have more than they need or can ever use. Cultural, economic, social, educational, and political factors play such key roles in social equity that it is easy to say placemaking is not a social equity issue. Yet places can support access and opportunity or create barriers. As architect Roslyn Lindheim wrote, "The design of the built environment constantly reminds us of our position in every hierarchy. The size and quality of space have always been indicators of social status, whether it is the size of a house,

Figure 12.1 *(facing page)*
North Beach Branch Library, Leddy Maytum Stacy Architects, Donald Corner, photographer

the exclusivenesss of a neighborhood, or the proximity to a window in an office building."[2]

The Public Library

The public library is an institution that stands out in its efforts to foster social equity. Public libraries today are arguably the most equitable of American public institutions. They provide free access to knowledge for all. People can study, read the newspapers, go to story hour with their children, listen to music, use a computer, surf the Internet, relax, sleep, or just shelter from the weather.

The first libraries, however, were only for the wealthy and the few. A place like the Laurentian Library, Florence, Italy, was built to house the few extant books, many handwritten by scribes in monasteries. Scholars and distinguished visitors, mostly men, were allowed access to the books. This model of libraries continued as the norm, even after printing presses began to produce many more books.

Free community libraries developed in the United States during the nineteenth century. These libraries, though often sponsored by wealthy patrons like industrialist Andrew Carnegie, were open to everyone. Women and children, as well as men, used the new libraries. There were grumbles about women in the library: "They are disruptive of serious library users. Constantly talking and giggling."[3]

More recently, those complaints were of teens in the library, although today's libraries willingly welcome teens with their own places. Architect Will Bruder in designing Phoenix's Burton Barr Central Library learned how to make an effective teen room by talking with teens. Teens did not want to be near the children's section. They wanted multiple kinds of informal places for sitting, lying on the carpet, gathering, and just being alone. Computers were essential. Wary teens wanted to cruise the place and check things out before committing to spending time there. In Phoenix, teens now use the library more than any other group.

Stories about libraries are many. A Berkeley librarian tells the story of bringing graham crackers and milk for children, knowing she is providing after-school daycare for some families. A Buffalo librarian told the story of how during the Depression, she noticed one man who came every day to the library, where he spent the whole day. One morning he came in and and told her that she would not see him the next day. He wanted to thank her for everything. He had found a job.[4]

Today, libraries face the challenge of becoming the home base for backpacking travelers and the homeless, who find the library a safe refuge and a resource. The staunchly egalitarian Berkeley librarians did not want to exclude anyone, yet they could see that many of the local citizens were excluding themselves. The homeless can fill reading rooms, dominate bathrooms, and practice imperfect hygiene

Figure 12.2
Pre-school classroom, Chicago, Studio Gang, Steve Hall, photographer

and other habits that drive families out of the central library and into the branches. In a renovation of Berkeley City Library, architect Cynthia Ripley improved the ability of that library to serve multiple, very diverse communities by dispersing stacks, reading tables and comfortable chairs throughout. People can now choose their spots and their cohorts, settle in, read, use a computer, just nap, or use the bathroom to wash up. Families and children are back.[5]

Public Schools

Like public libraries, public schools have a long history in America. The Edgartown, Massachusetts, School Committee Report of 1842/3 makes the case for public education. "For the purpose of public instruction, we hold every man subject to taxation, in proportion to his property . . . let children rich and poor meet together . . . [for a] lesson in republican equality, merit based for the future, where friendships and connections are formed."[6]

But schools have been fraught with inequality. They have a history of discrimination against people of different races, religions, genders, and abilities. In the United States, after the Civil War, there were few schools for black children. Educator and civil rights activist Booker T. Washington initiated a rural schools program, for which he found funding from philanthropist Julius Rosenwald. From 1912–1937, the program built more than 5,000 schools, workshops, and teachers' homes. African Americans contributed cash and in-kind donations of material and labor to match the Rosenwald grants. These buildings flew under the radar because they were vocational schools and included job training. Many gained access to education, and the buildings became community social centers. Although attacked and burned, these schools persevered, providing opportunities for thousands of children. Originally designed by Tuskegee

Institute staff architect Robert R. Taylor and then modified by others, the economic designs paid good attention to daylight and natural ventilation. Rosenwald schools are now designated National Treasures, for the opportunities they provided during a period of strict school segregation. There are proposals to preserve remaining buildings.[7]

Other inspiring initiatives to provide schools worldwide include architect Francis Kéré's schools in Burkina Faso and the MASS Design Group's Ilima Elementary School in the Congo. School building can be dangerous. In some parts of the world, terrorists have targeted girls who go to school and destroyed their school buildings.[8]

Location affects educational opportunities. Heather Schwartz, a RAND Corporation researcher, found that children do better in school if they attend school in a neighborhood not dominated by high poverty rates.[9] Montgomery County, Maryland, where Schwartz did the study, adopted policies dispersing public housing, so that many of the tenants attended public schools among a wealthier cohort. In another study, researchers found that the younger children move to better neighborhoods, the better they do.[10]

Schools make a tremendous difference and all too often still reflect the inequities in society. Some children are clever enough to thrive with limited resources, but not all. A visit to schools in different parts of most American cities is often all one needs to understand that school buildings can support or fail to support equity. In affluent neighborhoods, public schools may be well-equipped and maintained. In poorer neighborhoods, the message about the value of education is different. Windows do not open and close properly. Graffiti lingers on walls. Toilets are temperamental. Landscaping is poorly maintained. Many families in these neighborhoods no longer consider public schools a desirable option and, if they can find the means, pay for private schooling or send children to live with relatives in better school districts.

Size is another major placemaking issue for schools and is fiercely debated. As long ago as the 1950s, environmental psychologist Roger Barker argued that smaller schools support students more broadly than larger schools. All children are needed in smaller schools and all participate, because it takes quite a number of children to put on a play, staff an orchestra, or form a team. In larger schools, many lack opportunities, because only the "achievers" are needed. American schools have tended to get larger in the hopes of eliminating some administrative costs and including special educational opportunities. Many schools suffer from a high turnover of students. Children are dropping out at an alarming rate. When children do not finish a high school education, there are long-term costs for their own futures and for society as a whole.

In Finland, which has achieved top scores on international tests, K-8 comprehensive schools (*peruskoulu*) tend to be smaller than American schools. Pupils go to the same school for eight or nine years before selecting a high school, which gives teachers time to discover and solve learning problems.[11] The schools are community-based, attractive, and very well-maintained. The teachers are well-educated, respected, and well-paid.

Workplaces

Historically, patterns of inequity in workplaces have been highly visible. As people became more sensitive to status issues, the signals became subtler and required a bit of decoding. For example, if one were to visit a large architectural firm in the 1970s, at first glance, the one-hundred-person drafting room would seem to support everyone equitably. Yet, management, all white men, occupied glass-fronted, executive offices at one edge. Minority architects, mostly Asian American, occupied deluxe drafting desks with counter-balanced surfaces that could be raised, lowered, or tilted with ease. They were the drafters and seldom met clients. The few professional women (three out of one hundred architects) occupied sit-down desks with guest chairs and worked in the programming and concept design phases of the project. Women frequently met with clients, possibly because in the 1970s no one suspected that a woman would walk off with a client. Each position in that hundred-person architectural assembly line had a role that was reflected in its own assigned and distinctive chair, desk, and task light. For both women and minorities, strategy and tactics were required to get the broad experience needed to qualify for an architectural license. The place implicitly showcased inequality and reinforced it, although the management of this firm was comparatively progressive and did hire multiple women and minorities, unlike many others at that time.

The Organization of Women Architects queried many practices in San Francisco on their hiring during that same period. Many had no women in their offices for reasons recognized today as both offensive and illegal. One practitioner said there was only one grubby toilet for the guys that could not accommodate a woman. Another said he smoked cigars and women did not like the smoke. Few design practices today are ethnically or gender segregated. Discrimination still exists but is much less overt. The glass ceiling is rising, slowly. Architecture schools are typically half women today, and minority enrollment is increasing. Waggish design students have labeled the bathrooms "People," which addresses gender issues.

Universal Access

The successes of the civil rights and women's rights movements of the 1960s and 1970s inspired people with severe disabilities to take action toward greater social equity. Historically, at the University of California, Berkeley, these students were housed in the hospital, as the dorms were not accessible. The indignity of this accommodation was accepted, because unlike so many other universities, Berkeley provided at least some way for students with severe disabilities to live on campus.[12] The students formed a new organization, the Center for Independent Living, and engaged with other students from law, architecture, and planning, and with Vietnam veterans. They began to make demands for basic rights, not just accessible housing, but also dignified access to libraries and classrooms through front doors and not through service entries, past the garbage bins.

Little by little this effort led to the crafting of a civil rights act, the Americans with Disability Act (ADA) of 1990. Major changes in the way designers and builders conceive of accessibility to buildings, gardens, and even wilderness paths have followed. Building codes based on this civil rights act have made accessibility a legal requirement for any construction project. Requirements affect elevators, clearances for wheelchairs, ramped curbs at crosswalks, larger bathrooms, door swings, grab bars, safety warnings (visual and auditory), parking near destinations, and many other features. The efforts to upgrade existing places are ongoing. Universal access requires creativity as upgrades can be expensive, involve compromise, and conflict with historic character.

Too often solutions meet the letter of the code but lack common sense. Architect Fred Tepfer proposes asking four questions of every design solution: Is it universal? Is it effective? Is it welcoming and inclusive? Is it durable? A long ramp with numerous switchbacks is not equitable or welcoming, if everyone else only goes up a few front steps.[13]

Many of the early activists, who demonstrated even by crawling up the United States Capitol stairs, were mobility-impaired. In subsequent years, the definition of accessible

Figure 12.3
Edwards Community Center, Aloha, Oregon, Rowell Brokow Architects,
Christian Columbres, photographer

Figure 12.4
Site plan of the Aloha Project pocket neighborhood, Rowell Brokow Architects

---

Does this Place Foster Social Equity?

built form has evolved to better support access for individuals with impaired vision, hearing impairment, or behavioral disabilities like autism. And of course, everyone benefits: 75 percent of all Americans will have some disability by age sixty-four. Most will push strollers, pull suitcases, maneuver garbage bins, or use crutches at one time or another.

There are many around the country taking this work to the next level. The Edwards Center in Aloha, Oregon, built in 1972 by several families with children with severe disabilities, houses physical and mental therapy programs and offers job training and employment. The Center is dedicated to the independence and dignity of people with a variety of developmental disabilities.[14] As the original children are now adults, the families have begun construction of an inclusive pocket neighborhood, the Aloha Project, with a variety of housing for different combinations of people, including singles, small groups with a caregiver, and families. Each is universally accessible. As a first phase, the renovated center building is designed to draw people from the nearby community to come visit, enjoy the café and community garden, join in a yoga class, or have lunch. The idea is to "reverse integrate" the community. As the mission of the Center for Independent Living in Berkeley states, "The strongest and most vibrant communities are those that include and embrace all people."[15]

Housing Equity

Housing location and type both reflect and reinforce status in society and indeed, can create nearly insurmountable barriers to opportunity. A stable family house is often seen as the American ideal. Families without stable, decent housing face many problems. Frequent moves are disruptive, exhausting, expensive, and affect work and school performance. Mail may not be forwarded, and offers of employment may not arrive.

Without landlines, people rely on budget cellphones, "burners" with changing phone numbers. People may have to depend on families and friends and call on their resources inconveniently. Sharing housing may cause crowding and sleep deprivation. Nerves may fray, tempers flare, and marriages face challenges. A stable place to live in a decent neighborhood brings with it many benefits, but many are denied these benefits.[16]

When disaster strikes and people lose their stable housing, everyone feels the disruption, grief, and fear. The aid that arrives is often different for those with means than those without. The Oakland firestorm in 1991, that killed twenty-seven and burned 3,792 residences, was an upper middle-class disaster. The Red Cross arrived to help, providing coffee, doughnuts, cots, blankets, and other support, but only one family came to spend the night in the high school gym. FEMA (Federal Emergency Management Agency) offered help to the few uninsured, but good social networks, credit cards, and good fire insurance helped most. Several years later, people had rebuilt a majority of the houses, many of them bigger and better.

This story stands in sharp contrast to what happened to the low-income people in Louisiana, who lost their housing in Hurricane Katrina in 2005. This disaster was much larger and challenged FEMA logistics and capacity. More than 1,800 died, and damages were said to exceed 100 billion dollars. Many relocated to other cities. Many moved multiple times. For those in poor housing, their poor housing choices became worse. Years later, many still live in substandard, temporary housing. Housing and businesses have not recovered to pre-2005 levels.[17]

Migrant and refugee camps worldwide share these serious problems at an even larger scale. Substandard migrant housing can be accompanied by poor social support systems, poor access to education and health care, frequent moves, and exposure to crimes of poverty and historic enmity.

Designers asked to design a refugee camp face a moral dilemma. Is it better to provide some minimal shelter, even though these places isolate and stigmatize their inhabitants? Refugee camps are often seen as temporary, but temporary turns out to be a very relative term, as months drag into years and even decades for some.

People often yearn to help. They approach the problem generously. Many went to Louisiana bringing enthusiasm and unskilled labor, but longer-term commitments are necessary to solve problems of this complexity. In times of disaster, limited resources may be better used to give jobs to local residents with skills and to train others in rebuilding their own places.

Philanthropic aid is often contrasted with sustainable aid that builds community capabilities or social capital. Both are needed. Building capabilities can be as important as building the tangible parks, houses, schools, clinics, libraries. Habitat for Humanity, perhaps the largest developer of low-cost housing in the world, follows this principle. In the Habitat model, families seeking housing learn how to make houses and contribute to future housing in their communities. Families are carefully screened for home ownership and spend many hours at work on their new homes before moving in. Credit checks and education are part of the process. The worries of rent increases and landlords are replaced with the worries of paying the very modest mortgage and maintaining the house. In Oakland, the construction manager regularly explains to new homeowners with stopped-up toilets that he is not the landlord—indeed they are—and then offers the gift of a plumber's helper and a lesson in its use. Donations and sweat equity keep monthly costs below the cost of rent, and people develop building maintenance skills in the process. Habitat tells stories about the effects of home ownership. As one new owner said, "When you own your home, it stabilizes things ... Rentals are always unsure." Children do better in school, job performance improves, and residents get involved in community efforts. Habitat provides a good system that works well for many, but there are many more that need decent housing.[18]

Worldwide, many efforts, small and large, impact both the availability of decent affordable housing and community competence. Healthabitat, an Australian organization, founded by architect Paul Pholeros with a physician and an anthropologist and community organizer, has found that health outcomes improve in Aboriginal communities when houses are repaired. Simple improvements—fixing showers, clothes washers, and toilets; adding screens; intervening in the landscape to decrease dust; and grounding electricity—correlated with a 40 percent reduction in environmentally related hospital admissions.[19] Suffering and community costs have been reduced, and local people have gained skills.

Singapore is the rare place that has made a holistic national effort to provide its population with decent housing, which, by Singapore definition, is a four-room apartment in a high-rise. This widespread standardized housing upgrade has accompanied Singapore's rise into first-world status with a high median income level. One can argue that providing decent housing has provided an equitable basis for economic development. The whole story, of course, is much more complex. The unsung side-story in Singapore is the meager housing for guest workers from surrounding countries. While about 75 percent of resident families live in contemporary four-room flats, foreign workers may be housed eight to a dormitory room in converted industrial space, on shipboard, or in other expedient places. Some even sleep in shifts. These laborers have to leave loved ones behind in India, Bangladesh, or other countries.

Minorities in the United States have also experienced difficulties finding affordable housing or even obtaining mortgages when family prosperity allows. Many American banks have practiced redlining, limiting loan availability in minority neighborhoods. Prior to 1968, the "FHA [Federal

Housing Administration] *explicitly* refused to back loans to black people or even other people who lived near black people."[20] In many of these previously redlined areas, it is still more difficult and expensive to arrange a mortgage. Banks may still require immigrants and racial minorities to have better credit ratings and pay higher fees and interest rates. Single women have reported similar difficulties. These unfair patterns are changing all too slowly.

To make matters worse for low-income families, housing regulation has required new features over the years, such as minimum sizes for lots and dwellings, garages for cars, and other elements that lead to higher costs. Sixty years ago, a three-room carpenter-built cottage allowed a family to live very modestly in a mixed-income neighborhood near a good elementary school. Today, there are few American communities where this cottage could be built without adding a variety of features that would make it safer, more energy-efficient, possibly more durable, and, alas, less affordable. But more than that, the land to build a small house is now more expensive, less conveniently located, and frequently beyond even extreme commuting distance.

The character of the neighborhood is almost more important than the nature of the house or apartment itself. Neighborhoods have often been mixed, although segregation of various sorts has been common as well. Harvard economist Raj Chetty's study shows that where children grow up shapes their prospects as adults.[21] With GIS-based maps, researchers are beginning to see with detailed clarity strong correlations between place and opportunities to succeed.[22]

In Paris, the nineteenth-century Haussmann apartment buildings contained a slice of urban life: shops and offices on the ground floor, shopkeepers' dwellings on the mezzanine, wealthy people on the second floor or *piano nobile*, the bourgeoisie on the next floors, and in the garrets under the mansard roof, struggling artists and household servants. Everyone shared the stair hall and more importantly, they mixed in the street, the block, and the neighborhood. In Seattle, Washington, the hilly topography led to settlement patterns, where the rich lived in large houses on the top of the hills and the poorer in smaller houses in the valleys. Each neighborhood had a mix of family income, and neighbors sent their children to the same local schools.

Professor Mindy Thompson Fullilove describes how Charlotte, North Carolina, changed from a city in 1875 with mixed races and income levels throughout to a city that in 1980 had a very high level of both income and racial segregation. While urban gentrification may initially diversify segregated neighborhoods, higher prices quickly reach a tipping point, where poorer people can no longer live there. Today, urban gentrification is reducing diversity in many cities across the country.

New legislation in many cities is under consideration to maintain a mix of residents, including teachers, police officers, service workers, and other essential members of a functioning city, who are finding urban housing unaffordable.

Some cities have adopted regulations that respect renters' rights, making it more difficult to evict tenants as demand for housing grows and rents rise. Some cities require a percentage of affordable housing to be built as part of every housing development. In New York, there is controversy about where the mixing should occur. Developers for a luxury apartment building put the luxury entrance on a main avenue and the lobby for the required affordable housing on a side street. In the name of equity, should the two lobbies be joined? Or can the street be the shared public space?

Equity and Diversity

The subplot in equity stories is often cultural and religious. The oldest active synagogue in Europe is in Prague and has an intimate feel, with boxes for small groups of congregants,

Figure 12.5
Mosque arcade, Aleppo, Syria, Bill Hocker, photographer

not unlike early Massachusetts's churches. A central place for the Torah, rabbi, and cantor adds focus and immediacy. Then one notices that women are excluded from the intimacy of this sanctuary and have their own much smaller room at the back with a narrow slit for viewing the services. Similarly, sex segregation in traditional Islamic culture creates precincts for women at home.

What is the balance between cultural and religious patterns and discriminatory practices? How do places support both diversity and individual choice? These difficult questions, of course, cannot be answered simply. Converting a synagogue women's room into a crying room for parents and their infants may satisfy some, but for others, this would violate the religious requirement for segregation by sex. People choose places that reflect specific cultural and religious values. Places of social equity allow individuals to make these choices for themselves.

Is this a Zero Sum Game?

Paul Farmer is often cited as saying, "The idea that some lives matter less is at the root of all that is wrong with the world."[23] All too frequently, social improvements are pitted against each other. The movement toward social equity has been served by a wide-ranging series of interventions that are hard to coordinate.

News reports regularly contrast the spending on places for one group versus another group. Prisons and public schools, for example, receive grossly different dollars for construction, not to mention dollars for operation. It has been claimed that a year in prison costs more than a year at a four-year non-profit university.[24] Certainly the cost for one prison cell is much more than the cost for space for one preschool pupil. Why do these need to oppose each other? Both may be needed, although funding more places for Head Start and other early childhood schools could reduce the need to build and operate more prison cells. Community costs are often looked at narrowly rather than in the context of overall results.

There are some who think that market forces will take care of the inequities, although examples of this happening are few and far between. Most progress in justice has been achieved by the struggle of organized social movements. Today, social goals are funded and controlled more and more by wealthy donors, whom communities have not elected to make their decisions. Both public investment and public control in a democracy are critical.

The pursuit of social equity, of necessity, introduces a moral element. Are some more deserving than others? Is there a minimum standard that all should achieve? Does equity mean assimilating to the majority culture, or can places support and celebrate diversity in an equitable way? How can people remove barriers, open opportunities, and build competence? And for designers, how can placemaking contribute? Seventy-five years ago in his famous four freedoms speech, President Franklin Delano Roosevelt called out for civil liberties and opportunities for all: freedom of speech, freedom of worship, freedom from want, freedom from fear.[25] More than fifty years ago Reverend Martin Luther King, Jr. inspired many with his dream of equality.[26] President Barack Obama voiced it again, speaking to educators and students, "No matter who you are, what you look like, where you come from, you can make it. That's an essential promise of America."[27]

Notes

1   Paul Farmer, Jim Yong Kim, Arthur Kleinman, and Matthew Basilico, *Reimagining Global Health* (Berkeley, CA: University of California Press, 2013), xiii.

2   Roslyn Lindheim, "New Design Parameters for Healthy Places," *Places*, 2, no. 4 (1985): 21.

3   Quoted by Anthony Bernier in "A Landscape of Yes: Making Space for Teens in Public Libraries," conference presentation, Designing Modern Childhoods: Landscapes, Buildings, and Material Culture, University of California, May 3, 2002. "Ladies in Libraries," *Library Journal*, 11, no. 10 (October 1886): 420.

4   Margia Wilner Proctor, Deputy Librarian of the Buffalo Public Library, told this story to her granddaughter, author Jenny Young.

5   Ripley Scoggins Partners, architect Cynthia Ripley, planning and interior architecture, in joint venture with Bora Architects, the Berkeley Central Public Library, Berkeley, CA, 2002.

6   Jenny Young, "The Role of Schools in the Development of Urban Form and the Sustainability of Community Life," paper presented at the Sixteenth International Seminar on Urban Form Symposium, Guangzhou, China, September 4–7, 2009.

7   "History of the Rosenwald School Program," National Trust for Historic Preservation, retrieved August 28, 2016 at: www.preservationnation.org/rosenwald/history.html#Tuskegee.

8   "One-on-One with Malala's Father, Ziauddin Yousafzai," Plan Canada. Retrieved August 28, 2016 at: http://plancanada.ca/one-on-one-with-ziauddin-yousafzai; Nobel Peace Prize laureate, Malala Yousafzai was shot on a school bus on October 9, 2012. Her father, Ziauddin Yousafzai, shared the Peace Prize with her for his work as a journalist fighting for education for women.

9   Thomas B. Edsall, "Does Moving Poor People Work?" Opinion Pages, *New York Times*, September 16, 2014.

10 "Mapping America: Every City, Every Block," *New York Times*, retrieved August 28, 2016 at: http://projects.nytimes.com/census/2010/explorer.

11 Sahlberg, Pasi, *Finnish Lessons 2.0: What Can the World Learn from Educational Change in Finland?*, 2nd ed. (New York: Teachers College Press, 2014).

12 The University of Oregon pledged to reschedule any class so a disabled student could use one of the few accessible classrooms. They followed through on this promise with a heroic shuffling of classes the first week of each term, until they found the dollars to complete upgrading classrooms throughout the campus.

13 Fred Tepfer, campus project planning manager at the University of Oregon, website: pages.uoregon.edu/ftepfer/access.

14 Rowell Brokaw Architects, PC, the Edwards Center and the Aloha Project, Aloha, Oregon, 2012.

15 Center for Independent Living, formed in 1972 in Berkeley, California, www.cilberkeley.org.

16 Matthew Desmond, *Evicted* (New York: Crown, 2016).

17 Kim Ann Zimmermann, "Hurricane Katrina: Facts, Damage & Aftermath," livescience, April 27, 2015, retrieved August 28, 2016 at: www.livescience.com/22522-hurricane-katrina-facts.html.

18 Author Christie Johnson Coffin served on the East Bay Habitat for Humanity Board for many years.

19 Calla Wahlquist, "Paul Pholeros, Architect who Helped Reduce Indigenous Poverty, Dies at 62," *Guardian*, Australian ed., February 2, 2016, retrieved August 28, 2016 at: www.theguardian.com/australia-news/2016/feb/02/paul-pholeros-architect-who-helped-reduce-indigenous-poverty-dies-at-63.

20 Alexis C. Madrigal, "The Racist Policies that Made Your Neighborhood," *Atlantic*, May 22, 2014.

21 Binyamin Appelbaum, "Helping Families Move Far from Public Housing: US Voucher Program Sets Sights for Safer Neighborhoods," *New York Times*, July 8, 2015.

22 *New York Times*, "Mapping Poverty in America," retrieved August 24, 2016 at: www.nytimes.com/newsgraphics/2014/01/05/poverty-map; "Mapping the 2010 US Census," retrieved August 24, 2016 at: http://projects.nytimes.com/census/ 2010/map; Social Explorer (Oxford University Press, 2010), available online at: www.socialexplorer.com.

23 Posters with this quotation are widely available on the web.

24 California in 2009 reports spending an average of $47,102 per inmate in state prisons (retrieved August 28, 2016 at: www.lao.ca.gov/PolicyAreas/CJ/ 6_cj_inmatecost). In that same year the National Center for Education Statistics reports that average costs per student in four-year non-profit universities was $39,173 (retrieved August 28, 2016 at: https://nces.ed.gov/fastfacts/ display.asp?id=76).

25 Franklin Delano Roosevelt, "State of the Union Speech," January 6, 1941.

26 Martin Luther King, "I Have a Dream," Washington, DC, August 28, 1963.

27 Barack Obama, remarks by the President at the College Opportunity Summit, Ronald Reagan Building, Washington, DC, December 4, 2014.

Afterword

Design is a social art. People are complicated and knowledge about their relationships with the built world is full of ambiguity. As designers we question, but ultimately we commit to answers, selecting sites, forms, and materials and working with builders to complete places for people to use, enjoy, and ultimately change to meet their particular needs. Built places endure and tell their own stories. We hope that the stories that we tell last beyond us. We hope that over time the places we make will become places of utility and delight, where other people's stories unfold.

Figure 13.1
Watching the annual rodeo, Equador, Noelle E. Jones, photographer

What will your story be? Designers, builders, and community members all have the power to make choices. Every one of us has limited time and energy to make contributions to the world and a responsibility to decide where to devote our knowledge and ability. If you are a designer, with whom will you work? On which projects will you work? You may not be able to control all the decisions, but how can you make a difference? You can decide to quit when you believe projects are not supporting larger human goals. You can push for better decisions.

In the interconnected global world, there is little doubt about the inequalities. The vast majority of the world's population lives in places with poor access to good food, potable water, safe shelter, education, health care and equitable political processes. Where resources are limited, the imagination and creativity of design can make a difference. We encourage not just designers and builders, but community members and leaders to explore the complex social questions of our time and work toward answers that will make this a better world for all of us.

Christie Johnson Coffin
Berkeley, California
Jenny Young
Eugene, Oregon

Bibliography

Alexander, Christopher, Murray Silverstein, Shlomo Angel, Sara Ishikawa and Denny Abrams. *The Oregon Experiment.* New York: Oxford University Press, 1975.

Alexander, Christopher, Sara Ishikawa, Murray Silverstein with Max Jacobson, Ingrid Fiksdahl-King, and Shlomo Angel. *A Pattern Language.* New York: Oxford University Press, 1977.

Alexander, Christopher. *The Timeless Way of Building.* New York: Oxford University Press, 1979.

Alexievich, Svetlana. *Voices from Chernobyl: The Oral History of a Nuclear Disaster.* Translation and preface by Keith Gessen. New York: Picador 2005. First published 1997 in Russian as *Tchernobylskaia Molitva* by Editions Ostojie. First published in the United States by Dalkey Archive Press.

Angel, Lawrence J. "Health as a Crucial Factor in the Changes from Hunting to Developed Farming in the Eastern Mediterranean." In *Paleopathology at the Origins of Agriculture*, edited by Mark N. Cohen and George J. Armelagos. New York: Academic Press, 1984: 51–73.

Appleyard, Donald. *Liveable Streets.* Berkeley, CA: University of California Press, 1981.

Barker, Roger G., and Paul V. Gump. *Big School, Small School: High School Size and Student Behavior.* Stanford, CA: Stanford University Press, 1964.

Bateson, Mary Catherine. *With a Daughter's Eye: A Memoir of Margaret Mead and Gregory Bateson.* New York: W. Morrow, 1984.

Benedikt, Michael. *For an Architecture of Reality.* Santa Fe, NM: Lumen, 1992.

Bhatia, Gautam. *Punjabi Baroque and Other Memories of Architecture.* New York: Penguin Books, 1994.

Black, John R. *The Toyota Way to Healthcare Excellence: Increase Efficiency and Improve Quality with Lean.* Chicago, IL: Health Care Administration Press, 2008.

Boo, Katherine. *Behind the Beautiful Forevers: Life, Death, and Hope in a Mumbai Undercity.* New York: Random House, 2012.

Brand, Stewart. *How Buildings Learn: What Happens After They're Built.* New York: Viking, 1994.

Brill, Michael, with Stephen T. Margulis, Ellen Konar, and BOSTI. *Using Office Design to Increase Productivity*, 2 vols. Buffalo, NY: Workplace Productivity, Westinghouse Furniture Systems, 1984.

Brill, Michael, Sue Weidermann, and BOSTI Associates. *Disproving Widespread Myths about Workplace Design.* Jasper, IN: Kimball International, 2000.

Buder, Stanley. "The Model Town of Pullman: Town Planning and Social Control in the Gilded Age," *Journal of the American Institute of Planners*, 33, no. 1 (January 1967): 2–10.

Carey, John, and Public Architecture (Eds.), *The Power of Pro Bono: 40 Stories about Design for the Public Good by Architects and their Clients*. New York: Metropolis Books, 2010.

Cervero, Robert, and Erick Guerra. "Urban Densities and Transit: A Multi-Dimensional Perspective." Berkeley, CA: UC Berkeley Center for Future Urban Transport, 2011. Working Paper UCB-ITS-VWP-2011-6.

Chang, Shenglin Elijah. *The Global Silicon Valley Home: Lives and Landscapes within Taiwanese-American Trans-Pacific Culture*. Palo Alto, CA: Stanford University Press, 2006.

Chapin, Ross. *Pocket Neighborhoods, Creating Small-Scale Community in a Large-Scale World*. New Town, CT: Taunton Press, 2011.

Coffin, Christie Johnson. "Architectural Considerations for Designing, Constructing or Renovating Eye Care Facilities for High Quality, Large Volume, Sustainable Cataract Surgery." Architectural Module for the *Quality Cataracts Series*. Madurai, Tamil Nadu, India: Aravind/Seva Publications, 2001.

Coffin, Christie Johnson, "Thick Buildings," *Places*, 9, no. 3 (1995): 70–75.

Coffin, Christie Johnson, "Making Places for Scientists," *Places* 7, no. 4 (1992): 38–49.

Congress of New Urbanism and Emily Talen. *Charter of the New Urbanism*, 2nd ed. New York: McGraw Hill, 2013.

Cranz, Galen, Amy Taylor, and Anne-Marie Broudehoux, with John Ruble. "Community and Complexity on Campus and How to Grow a Business School." *Places* 11, no. 1 (1997): 38–51.

Cranz, Galen. *Ethnography for Designers*. New York and London: Routledge, 2016.

Dannenberg, Andrew L., Howard Frumkin, and Richard J. Jackson (Eds.), *Making Healthy Places*. Washington, DC: Island Press, 2011.

Den Hartog, Harry. "Shanghai New Towns: Searching for Community and Identity in a Sprawling Metropolis." Paper from the 4th International Conference of the International Forum on Urbanism. Delft, Netherlands, 2009.

Desmond, Matthew. *Evicted, Poverty and Profit in the American City*. New York: Crown, 2016.

Duffy, Francis. *The New Office*. London: Conran Octopus, 1999.

Dunham-Jones, Ellen, and June Williamson, *Retrofitting Suburbia*. Hoboken, NJ: Wiley, 2011.

Ellis, Russell, and Dana Cuff. *Architects' People*. New York: Oxford University Press, 1989.

Farmer, Paul, Jim Yong Kim, Arthur Kleinman, and Matthew Basilico. *Reimagining Global Health*. Berkeley, CA: University of California Press, 2013.

Fathy, Hassan. *Architecture for the Poor: An Experiment in Rural Egypt*. Chicago, IL: University of Chicago, 1976. First printed in 1973. Original publication in 1969 in Cairo, Egypt.

Franck, Karen A., and Teresa von Sommaruga Howard. *Design Through Dialogue: A Guide for Clients and Architects*. New York: Wiley, 2010.

Frumkin, Howard, Lawrence Frank, and Richard Jackson. *Urban Sprawl and Public Health: Designing, Planning, and Building for Healthy Communities*. Washington, DC: Island Press, 2004.

Fullilove, Mindy Thompson, MD. *Urban Alchemy: Restoring Joy in America's Sorted-Out Cities*. New York: New Village Press, 2013.

Gans, Herbert. *The Urban Villagers: Group and Class in the Life of Italian-Americans*. New York: Free Press of Glencoe, 1962.

Gardner, Howard. *Frames of Mind, The Theories of Multiple Intelligences*, 3rd ed. New York: Basic Books, 2011. With a new introduction by the author. First published in 1983.

Gawande, Atul. "Hellhole." *New Yorker*, March 30, 2009.

Gehl, Jan, and Birgitte Svarre. *How to Study Public Life*. Translation by Karen Ann Steenhard. Washington, DC: Island Press, 2013.

Gifford, Robert. *Environmental Psychology: Principles and Practice*, 2nd ed. Boston, MA: Allyn & Bacon, 1987.

Greenberg, Jerald, and Robert A. Baron. *Behavior in Organizations: Understanding and Managing the Human Side of Work*, 4th ed. Boston, MA: Allyn & Bacon, 1993.

Habrakan, N. John, J. T. Boekholt, P. J. M. Dinjens, and Sue Gibbons (Eds.), *Variations: The Systematic Design of Supports*. Cambridge, MA: Laboratory of Architecture and Planning, 1976.

Hall, Edward T. *The Hidden Dimension*. New York: Anchor, 1990. First published 1966 by Doubleday.

Hall, Edward T. *The Silent Language*. New York: Doubleday, 1959.

Hamilton, D. Kirk, and Mardelle McCuskey Shepley, *Design for Critical Care: An Evidence Based Approach,* London and New York: Routledge, 2009.

Harris, Marvin. *Cows, Pigs, Wars, and Witches: The Riddles of Culture*, New York: Vintage, 1989. First printed in 1974.

Helphand, Kenneth. *Defiant Gardens: Making Gardens in Wartime*. San Antonio, TX: Trinity University Press, 2006.

Hertzberger, Herman. "Shaping the Environment." In *Architecture for People*, edited by Byron Mikellides. New York: Holt, Rinehart & Winston, 1980: 38–40.

Hertzberger, Herman. *Lessons for Students in Architecture*. Translated from the Dutch by Ina Rike. Rotterdam: Uitgeverij 010 Publishers, 1991.

Hertzberger, Herman. *Space and the Architect: Lessons in Architecture 2*. Rotterdam: Uitgerverij 010 Publishers, 010, 2000.

Heschong, Lisa, Robert L. Wright, and Stacy Okura. "Daylighting Impacts on Human Performance in School," *Journal of the Illuminating and Engineering Society*, 31, no. 2 (Summer 2002): 101–114.

Heschong, Lisa, Robert L. Wright, and Stacy Okura. "Daylighting Impacts on Retail Sales Performance," *Journal of the Illuminating and Engineering Society*, 31, no. 2 (Summer 2002): 21–25.

Heschong, Lisa. *Windows and Classrooms: A Study of Student Performance and the Indoor Environment*. California Energy Commission Report. October 2003. Retrieved August 28, 2016 at: www.energy.ca.gov/2003publications/CEC-500-2003-082/CEC-500-2003-082-A-07.PDF.

Jacobs, Jane. *The Death and Life of Great American Cities*. New York: Vintage Books, Random House, 1961.

Kembel, Steven W., Evan Jones, Jeff Kline, Dale Northcutt, Jason Stenson, Ann M. Womak, Brendan J. M. Bohannan, G. Z. Brown, and Jessica L. Green. "Architectural Design Influences the Diversity and Structure of the Built Environment Microbiome." *ISME Journal*, 6 (2012): 1469–1479. doi: 10.1038/ismej.2011.211.

Koch, Ebba, and Richard André Barraud. *The Complete Taj Mahal: And the Riverfront Gardens of Agra*. London: Thames & Hudson, 2006.

Konnikova, Maria, "The Open-Office Trap." *New Yorker*, January 7, 2014.

Kroll, Lucien, and Peter Blundell Jones. *The Architecture of Complexity*. Cambridge, MA: Massachusetts Institute of Technology, 1987.

Kunstler, James Howard. *The Geography of Nowhere: The Rise and Decline of America's Man-Made Landscape*. New York: Simon & Schuster, 1993.

Lang, Jon T. "Privacy, Territoriality, and Personal Space: Proxemic Theory." In *Creating Architectural Theory: The Role of the Behavioral Sciences in Environmental Design*, 145–156. New York: Van Nostrand Reinhold, 1987.

Leaman, Adrian, and Bill Bordass. "Are Users More Tolerant of 'Green' Buildings?" *Building Research & Information*, 35, no. 6 (2007): 662–673.

Lee, Dorothy. *Freedom and Culture*. Upper Saddle River, NJ: Prentice Hall, 1959.

Lepik, Andres, and Barry Bergdoll. *Small Scale, Big Change: New Architectures of Social Engagement*. New York: Museum of Modern Art, 2010.

Lindheim, Roslyn. "New Design Parameters for Healthy Places." *Places*, 2, no. 4 (1985): 17–27.

Lindheim, Roslyn, Helen H. Glaser and Christie Coffin. *Changing Hospital Environments for Children*. Cambridge, MA: Harvard University Press, 1972.

Lynch, Kevin. *The Image of the City*. Cambridge, MA: MIT Press, 1960.

Madrigal, Alexis C. "The Racist Policies that Made Your Neighborhood." *Atlantic*, May 22, 2014.

Marcus, Clare Cooper. *House as a Mirror of Self: Exploring the Deeper Meaning of Home*. Berkeley, CA: Conari Press, 1995.

Marcus, Clare Cooper. "The House as Symbol of the Self." In *Designing for Human Behavior: Architecture and the Behavioral Sciences*, edited by Jon T. Lang. Stroudsburg, PA: Dowden, Hutchinson & Ross, 1974: 130–146.

MASS Design Group. *Empowering Architecture: The Butaro Hospital, Rwanda*. Boston, MA: MASS Design Group, 2011.

Montgomery, Charles. *Happy City, Transforming our Lives through Urban Design*. New York: Farrar, Straus and Giroux, 2013.

Monty Python, "Architects Sketch," Episode 17, *Monty Python's Flying Circus*, recorded September 18, 1970 and originally aired October 20, 1970, filmed as part of John Cleese's business management films series. Retrieved 27 August, 2016 at: www.youtube.com/watch?v=DyL5mAqFJds.

National Trust for Historic Preservation. "History of the Rosewald School Program." Retrieved August 28, 2016 at: www.preservationnation.org/rosenwald/history.html#Tuskegee.

Newman, Oscar. *Creating Defensible Space*. Washington, DC: US Dept. of Housing and Urban Development, Office of Policy Development and Research, 1996.

Nightingale, Florence. *Notes on Nursing: What it Is, and What it Is Not*. Kindle locations: 1668–1670. First published in 1859.

Norberg-Schulz, Christian. *Genius Loci: Toward a Phenomenology of Space*. New York: Rizzoli, 1979.

Norwich, William, "Sex and Real Estate," *New York Times Magazine*, June 1, 2003.

Owen, David. "Green Manhattan." *New Yorker*. October 18, 2004.

Owen, David. *The Conundrum: How Scientific Innovation, Increased Efficiency, and Good Intentions Can Make our Energy and Climate Problems Worse*. New York: Riverhead Books, 2011.

Postrel, Virginia. *The Substance of Style: How the Rise of Aesthetic Value is Remaking Commerce, Culture and Consciousness*. New York: Harper Perennial, 2004.

Preiser, W. F. E., H. Z. Rabinowitz, and E. T. White. *Post Occupancy Evaluation*. New York: Van Nostrand Reinhold, 1998.

Rangan, V. Kasturi. "Aravind Eye Hospital, Madurai, India: In Service to Sight." *Harvard Business School Case*, April 1, 1993, revised May 15, 2009.

Razani, Nooshin, Joan F. Hilton, Bonnie L. Halpern-Felsher, Megumi J. Okumura, Holly E. Morrell, and Irene H. Yen. "Neighborhood Characteristics and ADHD: Results of a National Study." *Journal of Attention Disorders*, 19, no. 9 (September 2015): 731–740. doi: 10.1177/1087054714542002.

Razani, Nooshin, and June M. Tester. "Childhood Obesity and the Built Environment." *Pediatric Annals* 39, no. 3 (March 2010): 133–139. doi: 10.3928/00904481–20100223–04.

Riis, Jacob A. *How the Other Half Lives: Studies among the Tenements of New York.* New York: Charles Scribner's Sons, 1890. Edited with an introduction by David Leviatin. Boston: Bedford/St. Martin's, 1996.

Robert Wood Johnson Foundation. "#CloseHealthGaps." Produced by the Virginia Commonwealth University Center of Society and Health. Other pertinent studies can be found on the RWJF website: www.rwjf.org/en/library/infographics/life-expectancy-maps.html.

Robbins, Paul. *Lawn People: How Grasses, Weeds, and Chemicals Make Us Who We Are.* Philadelphia, PA: Temple University Press, 2007.

Schlossberg, Marc, John Rowell, Dave Amos, and Kelly Sanford. *Rethinking Streets.* Eugene, OR: Sustainable Cities Initiative, University of Oregon, 2013.

Schweitzer, Marc, Laura Gilpin, and Susan Frampton. "Healing Spaces: Elements of Environmental Design that Make an Impact on Health," *Journal of Alternative and Complementary Medicine*, 10, Suppl. 1 (2004): S71–S83.

Settis, Salvatore. *Se Venezia Muore.* Turin, Italy: Einaudi, 2014.

Sheridan, Mike. "The Bay Area's Experimentation with Solving for Housing Affordability." *Urban Land: Magazine of the Urban Land Institute.* October 19, 2015. Retrieved August 25, 2016 at: http://urbanland.uli.org/planning-design/bay-areas-experimentation-solving-housing-affordability.

Skenazy, Lenore. *Free Range Kids, How to Raise Safe, Self-Reliant Children (Without Going Nuts with Worry).* Hoboken, NJ: Jossey-Bass, 2010.

Sommer, Robert. "Theoretical Influences," in *Social Design: Creating Buildings with People in Mind*, 34–49. Upper Saddle River, NJ: Prentice Hall, 1983.

Sommer, Robert. *Tight Spaces: Hard Architecture and How to Humanize It.* Upper Saddle River, NJ: Prentice Hall, 1974.

State of the Nation's Housing 2015. Joint Center for Housing Studies of Harvard University, 2015.

Suhr, Jim. *The Choosing by Advantages Decisionmaking System.* Westport, CT: Praeger, 1999.

Sweet, Victoria, MD. *God's Hotel.* New York: Riverhead, 2012.

Tilley, Alvin R., and Henry Dreyfuss Associates. *The Measure of Man and Woman: Human Factors in Design*, rev. ed. Hoboken, NJ: Wiley, 2001.

Tuan, Yi-Fu. *Space and Place: The Perspective of Experience.* Minneapolis, MN: University of Minnesota Press, 1977.

Ulrich, Roger S. "View through a Window May Influence Recovery from Surgery." *Science* 224, no. 4627 (1984): 420–421.

United States General Service Administration (GSA), Office of Government Policy, Office of Real Property Management, Performance Management Division, "Workspace Utilization and Allocation Benchmark." Retrieved August 25, 2016 at: www.gsa.gov/graphics/ogp/Workspace_Utilization_Banchmark_July_2012.pdf.

Weisman, Gerald. "Designing to Orient the User." *Architecture, the AIA Journal*, 78, no. 10 (1989): 109–110.

Whyte, William H. *The Social Life of Small Urban Spaces*. New York: Project for Public Spaces, 1980. Retrieved August 25, 2016 at: www.pps.org/reference/wwhyte.

Wolch, Jennifer R., and Michael J. Dear. *Malign Neglect: Homelessness in an American City*. San Francisco, CA: Jossey-Bass, 1994.

World Bank. *Migration and Remittances Factbook 2011*, 2nd ed. Compiled by Dilip Ratha, Sanket Mohapatra, and Ani Siwal of the Development Prospects Group. Washington, DC: World Bank, 2010.

Young, Jenny, and Anna Liu. *Five Years Later: Lessons Learned from Two Early Childhood Centers*. February 2013. Available from author on request.

Zeisel, John. *Inquiry By Design: Environment/Behavior/Neuroscience in Architecture, Interiors, Landscape, and Planning*, rev. ed. New York: W.W. Norton, 2006.

Zumthor, Peter, Maureen Oberli-Turner, and Catherine Schelbert. *Thinking Architecture*. Basel: Birkhäuser, 2006.

Figures

Index
